MOMENTUM

Kindle Direct Publishing

Las Vegas, Nevada 89081

blusunproject@gmail.com

MOMENTUM

A Shadow Work Guide & Journal

Quinn Barbour

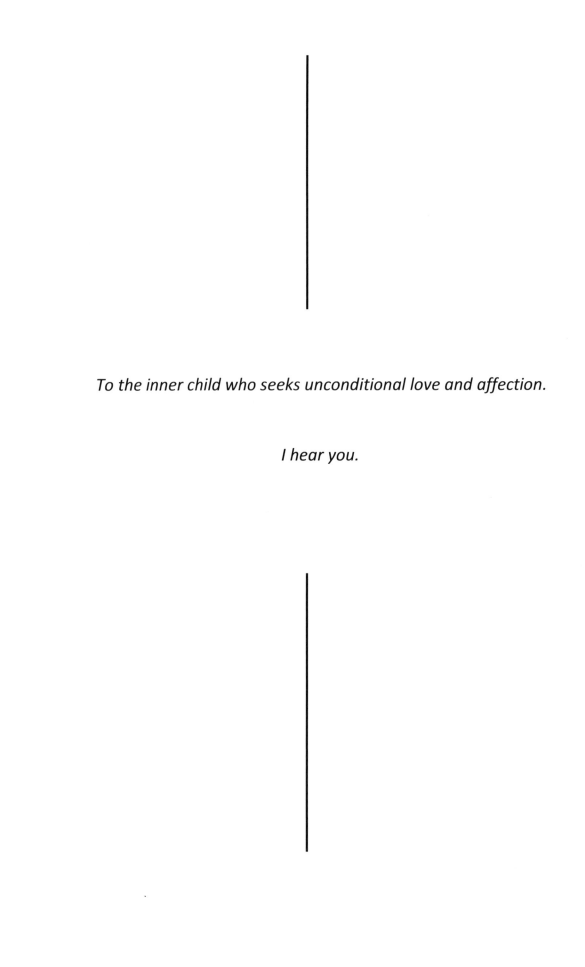

To the inner child who seeks unconditional love and affection.

I hear you.

This is for every **HUMAN** that begs for healing, whether knowingly or unknowingly. This was written to give you *strength* and resilience!

YOU ARE POWERFUL and this journal will show you just how bad ass you are! If you allowed this book to flow into your life, know it was written just for you.

D

E

D

I

C

A

T

I

O

N

CONTENTS |

PREFACE

It did not take  long for the idea of this piece to flow into my mind. I knew it was something that was absolutely needed if I wanted to see my community and the people around me get to a point in their life where they know that they are the creator of every single thing that happens to them, or should I say, FOR them. I wanted to give a gift that would keep on giving. I wanted to give you all something that would elevate and push you to the next level of growth that you may have thought you'd never reach. There are pieces of us that we want to hide because showing them to the world would only reveal our true selves; when showing them to the world may be what is needed in order to help heal the next soul that crosses our path. Revealing the shadows of an individual is a part of a massive snowball effect. Though slow to start, you have one person who is vulnerable and shows that, on one hand life is beautiful and there are no real complaints, yet on the other, if there are shadows that follow us around we will never truly get the life that we dream of and desire on a daily basis.

This is why I wrote Momentum, because I needed healing to be top priority in the lives of every amazing, dope, kick ass human being that currently exists and comes into existence (but we're going to trust that the trauma ends with us and doesn't fall upon babes)! I wanted people to know that with true, deep and raw healing, you can change the entire course of your life and the lives of everyone around you, even the generations that follow behind you. If you recognize your shadows, (I'll explain what Shadow Work is before you begin the work if you are unsure) accept them, love them and let…them…GO! This is the only way to spiritual freedom and wholeness; and with this journal/guide, you will experience many emotions. You will fall back into memories that you thought you suppressed, that you thought were forgotten about, not realizing the emotions you feel from them are obvious implications that your healing is incomplete.

I'm going to be completely honest with you, this is going to get ugly; but what is a storm if it isn't followed by the most beautiful rainbow and calming of skies? This journal will be the MOMENTUM you need to get you to where you want and need to be as a spiritual being having this wild human experience. It is filled with questions, challenges, space for you to journal and take notes, and tools and tips that can be used to aid in your shadow work.

IMAGINE THIS

YOU'RE IN AN OPEN FIELD, COVERED WITH
TALL WEEDS, SPOTS OF CRISP GREEN
GRASS WITH KISSES OF MORNING DEW
AND SPECS OF WILD FLOWERS THAT
SURROUND YOU. THE SUN IS BEGINNING
TO RISE AND GIFTS YOUR EYES WITH HUES
OF PINK AND ORANGE. FROM THE
HORIZON YOU SEE A SPOT IN THE MIDDLE
OF THE FIELD WHERE YOU CAN STAND,
ABLE TO FALL IN LOVE WITH EVERY ANGLE
YOUR EYES CAN TAKEIN. A FEELING OF
SERENITY OVERWHELMS YOU...MOMENTS
AFTER YOU FIND A PLACE TO REST, THE
SUN BEGINS TO SHOW FACE MORE
FIERCELY, CASTING SHADOWS FROM THE
WEEDS BEHIND YOU, BUT THEY DON'T
EXACTLY LOOK LIKE SHADOWS FROM THE
WEEDS..EACH OF THEM FORMS A WORD,
STANDING UPRIGHT, OVERPOWERING YOUR
SHADOW AND SUDDENLY YOU REALIZE
THIS ISN'T YOUR TYPICAL SUNRISE. THE
WORDS READ AS SUCH:

ABANDONED
ABUSE
UNACCEPTED
HATE
INSECURE
FEAR
NEGLECTED
BETRAYED
TRAUMA
UNLOVED
BELITTLED
HEARTBREAK
MISUNDERSTOOD

It's something you've never experienced before, a sight you almost wished you didn't see. Viewing the words before you that stole your childhood indirectly and kidnapped your adulthood without your awareness, were casting shadows all around you, giving you no choice but to face them and go through them. If you want to get out, if you're willing to revisit them and if you're willing to let them go. Here is a fair warning, on your way out of the shadows in this field, the shadows of the weeds and flowers you immaturely forgot about; the ones that, in a beautiful way, showed the darkness that lives deep in you, these feelings, emotions, regrets, etc., will have no choice but to touch you on your way to healing. They are on your path out and you must encounter them. This is where it begins, this is the journey towards wholeness.

66

Healing means gaining wisdom and understanding. The begining of soul elevation.

QUINN BARBOUR

Ready to change your life?

Let's begin...

VISION
BOARD

VISION
BOARD

ACCOUNTABILITY CHART

I WILL	BY

BUT WAIT...

WHAT IS SHADOW WORK?

Shadow work is a huge part of healing and evolving into our greatest potential. It is coming face to face with the parts of us we tend to hide from ourselves and from others. They are the pieces we pretend don't exist. The shadow is a direct reflection of our most hurtful wounds, the wounds that program our minds to believe we aren't enough, we aren't loved, and we are undeserving of our dreams.

Coined by Carl Jung, founder of analytical psychology

How

Psycho-cybernetics

&

Shadow

Work

Intertwine

*Our self-image, strongly held,
essentially determines what we become.*
-Dr. Maxwell Maltz

We all have this mental picture of ourselves that defines who we are and what we believe in. This mental film reel is a result from our past experiences, past successes, childhood traumas, past failures, and feelings and emotions. All things that play a part in the development of our personality. Psycho-Cybernetics is a psychological tool and phenomenal book written by Dr. Maxwell Maltz. Dr. Maltz served as an American cosmetic surgeon and author. He discovered his love for the mind by combining his daily work experiences as a surgeon with intricate studies in psychology. Maltz concluded that our self-image is foundation of our mental state, hence all the success and failures that happen in our lives as a result. The word cybernetics derives from a Greek term meaning *'a helmsman who steers his ship to port'.*

"Steering your mind to a productive, useful goal, so you can reach the greatest port in the world, peace of mind. With it, you're somebody. Without it, you're nothing". Dr. Maxwell Maltz

Since we didn't know what we know now in our younger years, we allow past experiences to define us in unfavorable ways. As adults we wind up behaving in a way that doesn't define who we really are at the core of our beings. This entire game is all about attempting to get you to comprehend that you can overcome any mental pretense that you have accepted for yourself. You can learn to adopt new experiences to ultimately become a whole new person. Occasionally, we forget that we are all placed here for a significant purpose and yes, we ALL have a purpose tailored to just us. Often, there are even significant lessons we must learn from the start; lessons of which we are born into, depending on how we left our last lifetime, and we tend to forget this huge piece of life. It's vital to keep in mind that you are THAT human, you are THAT person, that superb soul that has requested and disembarked on a journey back to Earth. It is your duty to express your greatness and learn the lessons so that you can showcase them to the world for a greater healing. It is more your duty to heal your soul and get to a place of understanding life, because wholeness is what this moment is about. Each person that graces the face of the Earth has the potential to become successful. They could receive all the things they've asked for, able to watch all their dreams unfold before their eyes. You can flow in pure happiness if you allow yourself the pleasure. Once you rid of thoughts of *"I can't", "I don't deserve this", "I'm not worthy of this"* or *"I don't value myself"* you can have full access to this opportunity of joy. Everything that encompasses negative self-talk should cease so that desires that are meant for you can flow into your space. The key to reaching this fresh way of thinking is to use that imagination that you may have left behind with your childhood. If we can have moments where we talk down on ourselves, being the bully we always despised, calling ourselves ugly, fat, unworthy, unintelligent, etc.; we can choose the opposite as well. We can create new mental images, new words and new ways of thinking if we begin to ACT as if we are already flowing within them. Act as if you are already successful, as if you already have the things that you want; as if you have the body and health you want, as If you already have the knowledge you want and so on.

Just simply, act as if. The reason we do this is because our brain cannot distinguish reality, your surrounding physical matter, from your imagination. When you close your eyes and listen to someone describing a red dog or a tall mango tree, you can easily see these objects being described through your mind's eye. Your brain doesn't know whether it is seeing them or if you are imagining them, it just can't distinguish the two. This is due to the brain only acting and reacting off the thoughts we send to it. Simply put, if we see something in the physical and we are processing what we see, we are sending it to our brain and then it is processed there, we can control this thought journey. Therefore, we can create new images for ourselves by telling our brain these new thoughts that we have about ourselves, and in turn, our body and brain have no choice but to obey us. It has no other option but to reconfigure those programs in our mind. The thoughts that we have that are no good for us become way too familiar and it's our duty to reprogram them into thoughts that are more ideal, the ones we really want to see unfold. We must get to a point of knowing we deserve everything that we've asked for. We must get into the habit of retraining our brains to accept these new programs, getting into the flow of consistency. Without consistency it simply will not stick. It takes 21 days to form a new habit and if we desire these new sets of programs we must commit and act as if our dreams are already present in our lives. This is the perfect time to conduct mental check-ins and body scans. You want to hold yourself accountable during this crucial time to be sure you are keeping up with the new programming and incorporating positive self-talk. It's also vital to see if you have reverted to your old ways of thinking and old habits; this is the purpose of checking in.

I will discuss meditation in the "Reflection" chapter, but during this time on your shadow healing journey it is essential that you sit with yourself. It's critical that you make your best attempt at disconnecting from everything that surrounds you and really work towards rewiring old programs and reconnecting them to new thought processes. You will often read in this book *"Take it easy on yourself and be kind to yourself during this process"*, because it will be a challenging one but a challenge that is doable. The importance of shadow work is to completely let go of all trauma, heartache, and everything we've been dealt in the past. Without letting it go there is no way to move forward into beings of knowledge and wisdom and of love and understanding. How can we heal the world if we cannot heal ourselves? We must begin with **US**. Without letting go you will always be the person you don't want to be.

Releasing the shadow increases your gain of blessings. Think about the amazing possibilities that will come about if you conveyed positive self-talk about everything that occurred in your life and everything you wish to do. No matter how grand the dream, if you want to own a billion-dollar company or help feed and house thousands, or let go of that trauma, you can do it. There will be that voice that swoops in whispering *"you're never going to be able to pull that off"*; but what if we changed that thought and began saying *"What if"*, or *"say I can do this"*, think of the possibilities. What if we finally got into the mindset of really saying *"I know I can do that"* and began doing the work, and in turn, be the very person who pulls it off. Think about how it would be to change those negative, destructive, traumatic thoughts into positive, successful thoughts. Imagine if this was the way of your mind daily.

Within Psycho-cybernetics Dr. Maltz speaks on when letting it go, you must also let go of any worry, any anxiety and any negative emotions that may be tied to it. You want to try to avoid these thoughts altogether. This will require hard work, hence shadow work. Let go of any expectations and allow yourself to have those subtle subconscious thoughts, those are the ones that are going to do the most work. Leave whatever it is that you've let go outside of you, and you will begin to see in time how the issues will show their reasoning and the problems will give us the answers. This is a time to embrace the concept of patience, because if you allow it, these things will work out the way it's meant for them to in due time. Let it go, give it a few day or weeks, and upon your revisit, you'll more than likely have the answers you sought.

Keep in mind we do live on Earth; we are human beings and we are here to have individual unique experiences. Problems and issues will arise, relationship disagreements will happen, but this is the only route towards wholeness. The experiences we have and the ones we are going to have will not always be happy.
Despite challenges, it's important to keep a positive mental state. This doesn't mean you should always be spewing rainbows and glitter, because that's not logical. It means that even in our state of feeling anger and frustration or anxiety, we must strive towards positivity being our base mental state. We ought to know that whatever it is that will occur for us is occurring for divine reasoning. It is presenting itself in our lives via a lesson and if it has shown up on your path, it is meant for you to grasp something from it. Whether it be a situation you deem as negative or one that is positive, it is your teacher. It's in your hands how you take it, either you accept it with negative emotions and energy, or you allow yourself to feel these human emotions, knowing with your soul that your circumstances are there for a reason. Maltz take us on a journey in Psycho-Cybernetics and speaks in detail on various visions and values when it comes to success with specific individuals. *They are as follows:*

Sense of direction | We are always in search of new accomplishments and ways to succeed; we want to become more than we already are and have more than we already have. This is the sole reason why goals and dreams are put into place and worked towards. It acts as a prerequisite for reaching success

Courage | be open to new experiences, new habits and new thought processes.

Charity | take others' feelings and emotions into consideration, not spewing hate or anger towards anyone because we are unaware of their situation

Esteem | Remember who you are during this process, be aware of your magic, that you have abilities to create everything and anything you want in this lifetime.

Self-Confidence | instead of focusing on the failures that you've had in the past, place your focus on all the successes that you've had. By doing this you are giving your brain a boost of motivation and in turn this push will lead you into more successful endeavors. This is the sort of thinking you do when reprogramming your mind.

Dr. Maltz also discusses failure mechanisms and how we should attempt to avoid them if we plan on living a fulfilling life. Remember some of these things will naturally come since we are in these human forms.

These failure mechanisms are as follows:

Frustration | disappointment will come, and we must learn to accept it in the moment and not be cruel to ourselves. These moments are only temporary, and they will pass. We cannot think of moments of frustration as long term, this is not their purpose.

Aggressiveness | This emotion can easily lead to misdirected aggressiveness and that can lead to disappointment. Positive aggressiveness, however, can show pure determination, allowing you to go for your goals without fear. Not giving into negative aggressiveness can help you tackle life's challenges. The opposing side will not lead to positive outcomes.

Insecurities | know and remember that you are great and worthy. Rid of thoughts that tell you that you are undeserving, you're not good enough, beautiful enough, deserving enough, etc. Having these kinds of thoughts are not going to get you to a place of success.

Loneliness | We all get lonely, but we do not have to sit in it. Having a tribe of people who love you is how we get through life, it's one of its greatest pleasures.

Uncertainty | Again, we are human, and we will make mistakes, without them there is no way to grow and learn, it's your job to gain knowledge and wisdom from them.

As you grow through Momentum you will see how significant Psycho-Cybernetics is to the process. Use the tips and tools given to you by Dr. Maltz and incorporate them into your shadow work journey. Having the knowledge of the two will lead you into a place of wisdom and understanding, love and healing, guaranteed.

66

"I embrace my shadow self.
Shadows give depth and dimension
to my life. I believe in embracing
my duality, in learning to let
darkness and light, peacefully
co-exist, as illumination."

JAEDA DEWALT

THE VOW

The best choice that you could have made was to pick up this journal and make a solid commitment to yourself. There is nothing more important than committing to something that will fulfill your life and give you the courage to take the next stride towards healing and bettering your future experiences; so, kudos to you for embarking on what will be a beautiful and impactful journey.

But before we go any further and start on this path towards healing, I want you to say the following vow aloud as a commitment to yourself and your soul.

The Healing Vow

"My healing is important to me, I have been through many years of giving and giving and many years of forgetting who I am, and I am now at the point where I have been led to myself. I am committed to taking hands with my inner child and loving the darkness within me, so that I can live the life that is meant for me to live. I understand that by NOT facing my darkness, I will continue to have pain and suffering for years to come. I also understand that if I face my darkness head on and I am shown a mirror of who I actually am, deep in the core of my being, true healing will begin, and all of the beautiful experiences I call upon and all the dreams I so tirelessly dream about will unfold like the birth of a sunflower right before my eyes. Therefore, I am committed to my healing, I am committed to this journey, I am committed to the ugly parts that will be shown as this journey goes on. I am committed to the beauty that will be taking place and I am committed to the change and the growth that will greet me along the way. If I ever feel fearful or uninterested in carrying on, I will revisit this vow and read it aloud, giving myself power and strength, and the push I need to continue my healing. Through this, I will be able to assist others on their path, become a better human for my planet and most importantly, I will remember to love myself."

Doesn't it feel good to commit to something that you know will be more than beneficial for not only yourself, but the people that are around you, the relationships you enter and the tribes you find yourself a part of, and our beautiful, forgiving planet?

Congratulations! You have just given yourself the responsibility to be committed to your soul's work. There is nothing more important that you can do for yourself than what you are doing right now. Now it is time to dive deep to discuss how this journey will look, what it will feel like and the changes that
will occur. Now that you are prepared to embrace your healing…

Let us begin…

> 66
>
> "Every pain, addiction, anguish, longing, depression, anger or fear is an orphaned part of us seeking joy, some disowned shadow wanting to return to the light and home of ourselves."

JACOB NORDBY

ACCEPTANCE

I trust you have been led here by the tiny voice in your head that tends to guide you to yourself. That voice that showcases your ability to think higher and love harder, is the voice that will begin to shape you into a being of constant awareness, shifting you closer and closer to your destiny. It's a large step to take, so consider yourself brave; because a lot of people do not and cannot make this choice. It's "too hard" for them and that's just where the road ends for most. There are no thoughts of *"I can do this*!" "I can control my emotions!" or *"I can heal myself!"*. No self-talk that heals, but only mirrored talk that destroys and keeps a person stagnant and confined to the prison of their minds. This will be an experience like no other, because you will discover a new you and find yourself in constant conversation with your younger self (lower self) and your higher self. It has the potential to get ugly and difficult to deal with, but an outcome so beautiful you'll be screaming *"thank you!"* to the emotions and situations you previously abhorred.

How exciting is it to know that just on the other side of fear, lack, abandonment, and neglect, lies a beautiful field drenched in pure happiness, healing, love and compassion because you've found the key that unlocks freedom! There are reasons for everything we go through. A quote from Michael Ledwith states "*We create our own reality every day, most find this fact hard to accept. It's easy to blame the people around us for the way we are. We place blame on everyone and everything around us. However we observe the world is how it comes back to us. The reason it's lacking joy, happiness etc., is because your focus is lacking in those things as well*".

It may not feel like it in the moment and life may feel like it's personally attacking you, but this is the opposite of what life is doing. These aren't just your thoughts solely, at some point, everyone has felt this way. We are more alike as humans than many may think. Our emotions, reactions and the way we are internally could be very similar to the person you pass on the street. The only difference is how each of you handle the cluster of thoughts and emotions that flood you daily and of course the masks.

Throughout this guide we will be focusing on our inner voice and being, the one that tends to hide him or herself from the world, but also the one who silences us in times when we need to stand firm. THAT person, will become your best friend and some of you may even feel it's your worst enemy, but this isn't the case. No enemy will force you into growth and evolution, in fact, they will do just the opposite and stunt it. So I encourage you, as you read this guide and do the work that comes with it, do not look at your shadow self as the enemy, as the one who is pulling out all of these nasty attributes that have been hidden for so long, that's not what the shadow is or its purpose in our lives. It's the greener side of the field, the one that's unfamiliar and unknown but desirable. It's the freedom you'll eventually learn to love because of your realization that it isn't here to harm you at all, but to help heal your dustiest and darkest corners.

There is only one real way to prepare for this journey. You just simply need to want it and do the work. I can give you a step by step list on how to begin (and I will, although steps vary and individuals may heal as they feel) but you must be the initiator, this is YOUR journey and YOU have to make the ultimate sacrifice to partake in it. After all, there are so many beautiful things waiting for you on the other side of healing. Everything you've ever asked for awaits you. The question is, are you ready for it? Whatever your answer is, be sure it's the answer that will push you forward. (In other words, you better be ready, it's happening regardless.)

A mindset of acceptance is important to have when beginning shadow work. A task that sounds so simple to do, but many find the first step the hardest. It's difficult for majority of people to own up to their hurt and admit that they act and respond certain ways due to having real wounds that are still very painful from their past. We have so many triggers before embarking on shadow healing. Many triggers that cause us to fold in circumstances that are uncomfortable and difficult to get through. Occasionally we can see the triggers clearly but it's often that we feel an emotional flood has hit us out of the blue. We have all experienced attitudes and traits about ourselves that seem to come from nowhere, leaving us questioning ourselves and who we are. Total identity crisis.

"Am I crazy?"
"Something must be wrong with me." or
"You brought this out of me!"
"I wouldn't have this attitude if it weren't for you". Ahhhhh victim blaming.   An unhealed shadows favorite sport.

As well as the very mindset that will keep you where you are in your life. Constantly blaming, being the victim and taking yourself out of every situation you caused, for others to baby and coddle you. Oh…you thought this guide was going to be a sweet guide with a little cherry on top?

Sweet doesn't make you act. Tough love will though, love that evolves you past your shadows, above your shadows and into a new light, and that's what you're going to get throughout this guide, because I need you to heal. The world needs you to heal. "Well why do YOU need ME to heal? What's that got to do with you?" You are me, you reflect me in this pool of humans and since that is the case, I need you to heal, so we can heal. You obviously desire it just the same seeing as how you've picked up this guide, aware of how it will change your mindset and transcend your emotions, because it will if you do the work.

There will absolutely be moments throughout this guide where you will want to say, *"forget this!"*, and moments of clarity and realization. There will be times where I will probably trigger something so hurtful in you, you may hate me, just for the moment though, because no matter what the assignment, it's to help you heal and you'll be able to see the effects of it. I can say it a thousand times, but you will not know until you are experiencing it, this will not be easy. Remember you are healing from years and years of hurt and pain that has been entrapped within your body. This is going to take time and most importantly, patience. Frustration will make itself seen and giving up will be a thought that crosses your mind from time to time. Do not quit. Quitting means you've neglected your purpose and have accepted the fact that you don't deserve better.

Acceptance is the work for this chapter. Once you reach the point of accepting the flow of your life, that is when the work can begin. Constant denial and avoidance will land you in a spiral of questioning and doubting your worth and things you know you deserve. Really believe you can do this and do not doubt, doubt will kill the affirmations and commitments you have given to yourself and source. Momentum is like the 12 step process individuals must make when on the road to alcohol or drug recovery. The first step is to acknowledge the fact that you even have a problem, because without that tidbit of information, you will continue to latch onto things that do not serve you. Remove the blindfold and sit through the revelation of who you are, who you really are, when the doors are closed, and no one can witness you be you. THAT is the person you will be working with throughout this journey.

Self-Guide

Questions:

What is it I'm wanting to heal from?
What do I want to heal myself of?
How have I healed in the past? Did it work for me?
Who is involved in my healing? (Herbalist, spiritual leader, etc.)
Where do I feel most comfortable and at peace?
What places can I go to help me heal?
On a scale of 1-10 how serious am I about my healing?

Homework:

Write a letter to your younger self and write a letter to your older self.
Letter to the person you feel hurt you the most or effected your transition into adulthood the most?

Affirmations:

I am healed
I accept my healing in whatever form it comes
I love myself
I love the people who hurt me, because they are making me a better person
I am loved
I am love
I am growing and evolving
I deserve to live out my purpose
I am resilient
I am persistent and consistent with my journey
By healing myself, I will heal others and Gaia

66

The shadow is a moral problem that challenges the whole ego personality, for no one can become conscious of the shadow without considerable moral effort.
To become conscious of it involves recognizing the dark aspects of the personality as present and real. This act is the essential condition for any kind of self-knowledge.

AION (1951).
CW 9, PART II: P.14

T R U S T

CHAPTER 4

CHAPTER 4

This process can cause several issues to come up, leaving room for many questions to arise and it will not be easy to accept; but at some point, acceptance is necessary. You will begin to relive situations and remember people that once caused you a great deal of stress and trauma, along with countless other emotions. This will undoubtedly bring up issues of trust: trusting the people around you, in your personal space, and trusting yourself. According to Erik Erikson's Theory of Development, we go through a period in our lives lasting from birth to around 18 months that establishes our view of the world, beginning with our parents. This period is the Trust vs. Mistrust stage. I won't get too technical on this topic nor will I go on and on with the details of this theory, but I find this stage crucial to the larger parts of our lives. It begins early and may seem mediocre in the grand scheme of life but as adults, trust goes lengths and it is vital to most, if not all, situations. As it's known with infancy, we learn to link the person who feeds us and cares for us as the person who we must trust the most or who we hope to trust the most, seeing that they do their "job". This is also where it can get sticky. If the caregiver isn't doing his/her job as a nurturing parent/guardian, this can lead to questions from the child and eventually a loss of trust in that parent, thus lacking trust with the world. It gets that big. It begins from something as "simple" as providing the basic needs for a child, to losing their trust completely with the world if that task is not fulfilled. It's a great deal of pressure on the provider when it's looked at from that vantage point.

Throughout our childhood and adolescence, we go through many phases of trusting the people around us and doubting if anyone we encounter can be trusted. The latter usually stems from poor relationships and situations where the trust was established, but unfortunately broken. This can lead to avoiding new friendships and relationships and an isolated life due to fear, but not just any fear. A fear of something that hasn't even came to life yet, a fear of being hurt by a person you haven't even met yet, a fear of a love you haven't even experienced yet. Think about it, you are swimming in an ocean of fears of certain situations and circumstances that literally do not exist. It sounds silly, but that little voice, your "lower self", is a victim to pain and refuses to allow another broken individual to swoop in and take the morsel of love we have left for ourselves.

You need to show fear the way out the door. It's your home, your thoughts, your body, your emotions and fear must not exist in the same space as power. Learning to be the controller of all things YOU is vital to moving into and pass this step. Accepting that people and things are meant to flow how they flow and leave when they leave is the key element in trusting. When you allow things to simply BE, you will come to understand that everything and everyone has their own path and whether that is to remain in your life or not, or whether to make the right choice or not, it must be accepted as THEIR truth.

Doing this will allow a flow of abundance to flood you, because there is a willingness to accept all things…as they are. This is true trust and love. This is possibly the most difficult stage to accept, but by far the most rewarding.

Self-Guide

Questions:

➢ Do I have issues with trust?
➢ Who in my life do I feel I can't trust? Why?
➢ Have I forgiven the people who lost my trust?
➢ If not, why?
➢ Do I trust myself? Trusting I will make the right choice for the betterment of my life? Why or why not?
➢ Have I attempted to let anyone new into my life or have I avoided building relationships due to fear?
➢ How can I change my mindset on trust?

Homework:

➢ Give something/someone a chance that before, you wouldn't have trusted. Feel it in your heart first before moving forward.
➢ You can also forgive that person that broke your trust. (don't roll your eyes just do it…for you)
➢ If neither of these are an option, write a note or letter to the person or situation saying whatever you feel. Do not send it. Burn it. Let it go.

Affirmations:

I am forgiving
I am forgiven
I trust that I am protected
I trust only love will flow to me
I love the relationships and situations that flow to me
I love the flow of trust that floods my soul
I love how accurate my discernment is
I deserve love and affection
I am powerful

Filling the conscious mind with
ideal conceptions
is a characteristic of Western
theosophy, but not the
confrontation with the shadow and
the world of darkness. One does not
become enlightened by imagining
figures of light, but by making the
darkness conscious.

"THE PHILOSOPHICAL TREE"
(1945). IN CW 13:
ALCHEMICAL
STUDIES. P.335

VALIDATION

No matter what anyone has said you have been right, your feelings are valid. Everything that you feel is valid. The emotions you feel, the ones that suddenly flow into your life or the ones that have been a regular visitor for some years, come to you for a reason. We're aware you didn't ask for this and you don't feel you deserved it, but this is something you need to know. You need to know that without them, you are a void, an empty, hollow, body with absolutely zero connection to the world. You need them, but a lot of us simply don't want them, because of the immense power they can hold and the control they seem to have over us.

Or the control you LET them have.

This is the time to accept them and allow them to flow to you. Know within your heart that they do not make you but feeling them is a necessity for your healing. The authentic, vulnerable kind of healing. The stupid cry and vomit screams. All necessary. Although, many people find themselves not wanting to show what they feel, therefore masking it and putting on a front just to satisfy the comfortability of others and ego. It isn't about them and the mask doesn't work. What hiding does is it digs a crater of emotions so deep that an explosion is inevitable. A moment will become too much, too fast and that will be the day. BOOM! You're in the middle of a disagreement about what's for dinner and you completely SNAP, and there it goes, all those emotions you hid for so long to protect your ego, right on the dinner table. The very thing you need to let go of is now the first course, an unappetizing one. And if you honestly believe that you are hiding any of these emotions, you're not. It shows in the way you work with others, the way you treat others, your level of solitude, where you are in your life, etc. It's even more obvious to the people that are around you that pick up on that sort of energy naturally. We feel you.

On the other hand, being vulnerable with these same emotions, the tough ones that would be a lot easier to hide, will only be beneficial. Being you, authentically, can even encourage more people to be open and vulnerable. Doing so will give people something and someone to relate to, someone who can walk through their day continuing to do what it is they need to survive but also feeling what it is that needs and wants to be felt. Do not allow embarrassing emotions and feelings of "they're looking at me" to stop you from letting that deep feeling be felt. This isn't the ok to begin losing control of your emotions in places or situations where it is deemed inappropriate but to encourage you to take the control yourself. You are the creator and you own this shit. Do not let it own you. Allow the hurt, anger, unhappiness, neglect, loneliness, etc. to be felt as if on a conveyor belt of feelings traveling through your body and aura, letting it flow in one end and out the other. Think about all the times you have felt these heavy emotions.

How long did they last? Were they only for a few minutes? A few hours or days? Did they eventually go away? I'm sure for most cases this is the result. It always goes away and you always at some point, end up feeling better. If you do not feel and then retire old emotions into knowledge and wisdom you are never going to evolve into a "soul-filled" person, a "soul-filled" person overcomes all adversities by taking control. So why not just allow them to be and wait till they're over and instead, ask yourself a few questions in the moment. Questions that I'll put in this chapter's assignment.

Self-Guide

Questions:

> - How worthy do I honestly feel I am?
> - What do I find value in?
> - Can I trust myself?
> - Do I accept or deny the situations I have been placed in? If I deny them, why?
> - Did my caregivers provide everything I needed as a child? Or did I lack in areas?
> - Have I trusted the people around me? If not, why is it difficult for me to build that trust?
> - How much does it affect me when people are no longer a part of my life?

Homework:

> - Be fearless with whatever it is you've been holding back on. Just do it. (with good intentions)

Affirmations:

I am worthy
I trust myself
I trust that everything that flows to me is for me
I trust my intuition
I have everything I need
I love myself and my company
I accept things that have happened for me

66

Taking it in its deepest sense,
the shadow is the invisible
saurian
tail that man still drags behind
him. Carefully amputated, it
becomes the healing serpent of the
mysteries. Only monkeys' parade
with it.

*THE INTEGRATION OF THE
PERSONALITY. (1939).*

'I AM IN CONTROL

ANGER

I AM IN CONTROL

Anger. A topic that is very touchy for majority of people because we find ourselves entering a space where we no longer feel like us and when we enter those spaces it almost seems as if we lose ourselves and our power. The number one feeling a lot of us don't want to encounter. However, while it's perfectly ok to express the emotion of anger in a healthy way, it can affect us in a way where it triggers old memories, brings forth past situations that may be sensitive for us and brings up issues that we don't necessarily want to revisit. Anger stems from the feeling of not having control and this is the case for a great deal of situations. When we lose control of something or if we feel that in some way, shape or form that we are being harmed whether physically or mentally, or in our eyes, disrespected, immediately some form of anger comes over us. Now this can go as minuet as being annoyed or frustrated to as dramatic as blackout anger, either way it goes, those emotions are 100% valid and 100% ok to be felt…in that moment. You have more than enough permission to be angry at the situations that you went through because they sat you in a pool of emotions you assumed you couldn't handle (although you did). There must always be a reminder that sparks the notion that the anger you felt THEN was valid and made sense for the situation that they stemmed from.

This begins to take a turn as we transition into adulthood and begin to become more aware of our ways, what we may have brought from that situation and how it affected us. We become less angry and more thankful because being in that space taught us more than we could have learned being in a space of pure, untouched happiness all our childhood lives. Going through situations that bring up dark emotions in us are the exact circumstances needed to be the soil that we need to grow and feed the flower that we dream of blossoming in to. The dark places had to exist for the light to find its way out and that is what we should be focusing our attention on. Our "bad situations" (which aren't "bad" at all in the grand scheme of things) and the circumstances that brought up so much anger and hurt and pain were the exact moments we needed to get to where we are now. Rather than being resentful towards the things that happened for you, not to, we must take on an attitude of thankfulness. Giving these situations love and understanding and gratitude will bring light to why they even happened in the first place. Think about it long and hard, if it hadn't been for these issues arising in your space would you be where you are? Physically and mentally? Think about how you would have flowed through life without them? Would you have learned anything or appreciated anything? Really take a moment to think about this, especially if you are reading this thinking it was a punishment and something that happened TO you. So, whilst anger is ok, it must be very fleeting. Treating it as a passer byer. Knowing that no matter how redundant and cliché it may sound, it happened for a reason, even the worst thing imaginable. Though difficult to accept, these are the truths of childhood and of course, even adulthood.

Anger probably should not be the FIRST emotion felt in a situation. If you are aware of your surroundings and the control you have over those fleeting emotions when a situation arises, stopping to think and react with love and logic is ideal. You must remember that in this case, in any case, you are present to learn a lesson, whether miniscule or grand. Take a step back, evaluate the situation, ask yourself is it worth giving the full energy of anger (the answer is no btw) or just a small moment, and then allow yourself to flow in the feeling of understanding, grasping the lesson that came just to be learned by you. Take back your power, this is where you stop allowing the past to affect your future, this is where you become light.

Self-Guide

Questions:

➢ From my childhood, what is the one thing that stands out that still makes me angry?
➢ Who did it involve?
➢ What about it, in detail, made you angry?
➢ Have you thought of why it may have happened to you?
➢ What did you learn from the situation?
➢ Have you forgiven all parties involved? Why or why not?
➢ If the situation still exists or even if it doesn't, do you still see it with the same eyes?
➢ When you get angry about it now, how do you cope?
➢ What sorts of self-talk do you engage yourself with when it comes to this situation?
➢ How often do you think about it? Do you feel your answer is excessive or just enough?
➢ Had you not been in the situation, how different would life be today? Would it have changed the choices you made?
➢ Have you fully moved on from this? If not, why?

➢ Have you spoken to a therapist or counselor? How did it help? What did you learn?
➢ How can you apply this knowledge so you can heal?

Homework:

➢ Write a letter to the person or situation. Don't give it to them. Burn it.
➢ Have one last deep cry about it. Let it be the LAST.
➢ Write or draw what the situation was, then on another piece of paper, write or draw how you could have looked at it from a standpoint of love and understanding. (Hopefully this will change the way you looked at it)

Affirmations:

I am forgiven, therefore I forgive
I am in control of every one of my emotions
I respond with love and compassion
I am understanding
I radiate light and love
I attract beautiful situations and people into my life
I am thankful for the lessons learned
I am the creator
I get back what I put out
I am a magnet for love

"

We carry our past with us, to wit, the primitive and inferior man with his desires and emotions, and it is only with an enormous effort that we can detach ourselves from this burden. If it comes to a neurosis, we invariably have to deal with a considerably intensified shadow. And if such a person wants to be cured it is necessary to find a way in which his conscious personality and his shadow can live together.

"ANSWER TO JOB" (1952). IN CW 11: PSYCHOLOGY AND RELIGION: WEST AND EAST. P.1

SADNESS

Your inner child needs to know and feel that there is nothing that they could have done to change the circumstances that eventually lead to traumatic and emotional adult experiences. After you have screamed, cried, punched walls, or however you choose to release, there comes a phase that we enter, sadness. We grieve the childhood that we lived and the childhood that we missed out on. We grieve the memories that shattered us, and we grieve all the losses we took as a child and unfortunately this flows over into our adult life. Most often without our awareness. We enter a type of silence that we feel no one will understand. Having these moments can easily spill over into self-blame, and self-blame could lead to shame and that shame can and will lead us further away from our higher self, our true self. Doing this can then lead to self-harm and abuse and doing things that we were "taught" by our abusers that we feel is the only way to escape what lies dormant inside. We talk down on ourselves, which in the grand scheme of obviousness means we're bullying ourselves, in hopes that maybe that will make us feel better or maybe that's just all we're used to hearing. Entering this time of sadness is very heavy and can be a lot for a person to endure. Although possible, it doesn't leave much room for the joy we seek. We must get to the point where we truly know that within ourselves, the only way to get out of any situation, is to feel our way through it. Most times these emotions feel so heavy and our minds and bodies so weak that we feel that it's unbearable to even approach the situation with open arms in order to heal it. It seems out of our reach, as if we are too weak to bring ourselves out of the hole we have made home.

The work must be done. Sadness will come, grief will come, all these dense emotions will come, but they are not stagnant, they do not have to build firm foundations in the coming years as you heal. This journal will be a useful tool to bring you out of that dusty, dark corner, out of the pool of tears you've been shedding and out of that skeleton filled closet you've been comfortably resting in. Without letting go of the shadow we continue to hold on to things that will not allow us to grow, this will be it, the life you have now...will be the one you'll always have. It's important to remember that the emotions we feel, especially the heavy ones, are just dense versions of our thoughts. We have control over them, this is your hidden superpower. It just comes to a point where we must convince ourselves of this phenomenon.

Sadness is inevitable when being a human, at some point we all feel it. It's within the yin and yang of life, the good and bad that balances the planet we thrive on, it's apart it all. The thing that you must control though, is the flow of it, how you sit in it, how you cope when it is present, the activities we participate in when feeling so deeply, etc. Do you allow it to affect your entire day, and not just the moment it's currently sitting in? In the larger picture, sadness is your light. There is only one place to go once you've hit your low point and the answer is obvious, the only direction is up. It's at the bottom of the staircase of emotions and the more steps you take upward, from one emotion to the next, will only guide you to a place of peace and bliss if done with love and understanding. BUT it is important that the work is done, that you are doing everything you can and taking the healthy risks in attempts to become better than you were. This is the greatest gift you can give yourself at this point in your shadow healing journey.

Self-Guide

Questions:

- ➤ Write an apology letter to yourself for all the self-blame and self-harm you've done towards yourself regarding the situation, so you were placed in as a child.
- ➤ What are some of the things you do when you are experiencing sadness? Does it help?
- ➤ What are some healthy ways to cope with sadness?
- ➤ How long does the sadness last when it does come? Hours? Days? Weeks? How can you bring yourself of it, so it is only brief?
- ➤ How do you have to talk to about how you are feeling? Are you always honest with them?

Homework:

- ➤ Write a list of healthy activities that will bring you out of your sadness.
- ➤ Spend a good amount of time in nature if possible.

Affirmations:

I am loved
I allow myself to feel my emotions and treat them accordingly
I love myself
I am free
I am growing and learning everyday
I am filled with happiness and joy
I am a powerful creator
I have total control over my emotions

Everything happens for a reason.

To confront a person with his shadow is to show him his own light. Once one has experienced a few times what it is like to stand judgingly between the opposites, one begins to understand what is meant by the self. Anyone who perceives his shad and his light simultaneously sees himself from two sides and thus gets in the middle.

"GOOD AND EVIL IN ANALYTICAL PSYCHOLOGY" (1959). IN CW 10. CIVILIZATION IN TRANSITION. P.872

FEEL

We try to stop it; we don't necessarily want to feel or see the heaviness of the memories and emotions from all the things that happened to us shoved in our face. We try to avoid feeling so deeply, unaware that attempting to halt the emotions from flowing into our being is doing way more damage than it is good. Perhaps some of these memories trigger us or maybe they bring up feelings that are too challenging to feel or maybe they go as far as physically making us sick. These are all feelings that make sense when it comes to harmful or unhealthy situations that entered our lives ever so slickly and changed it drastically, or not so drastically, but indeed changed its course. We may come to a point where we feel that we are now adults and that piece of us should no longer bother us as much as it does and that it should be suppressed, no longer existing in our minds. It becomes an extension of who we were as children and what situations we were placed in unknowingly. These things carry over into our adulthood so easily and effortlessly that sometimes it slips under the radar and we don't see that it's the soul reason we act and react the way we do. It's obvious that we are still carrying around the baggage from our childhood that was never healed, we never released it and never accepted it, therefore, treating it as another piece that must travel with us. Most of us would rather not enter a state of anxiety, depression and heavy emotions that will come along with healing these pieces of us that are very important to heal in order to become the forever growing specimen of GOD that we are.

Having feelings towards a situation is okay. When we are continuing to feel the emotions from the situation(s) it's just an obvious representation that we are still connected to those experiences that occurred in our past and that we have not let them go nor have we healed from them. If you are still feeling from them, you are not healed from them. In order to heal you must feel. Yes, emotions that are ugly will probably come up. Let them. Allow them to be like clouds floating by in the sky, flowing in and out of time and space. See them, accept them, love them for what they are and know that without them you wouldn't be as determined as you are now to heal them. Without feelings, it will be a struggle to get to the place where you desire to be, these things must occur, you must feel!

No one likes to feel overly emotional, it's almost taboo to most beings. Being tied down by tears is not ideal but the reason we are attached to these emotions is because they are attached to experiences and situations that we've dealt with and are still dealing with and that's why we feel we can't move forward. We feel the situations are already what they are, they aren't changing, and that they are a part of a past that will never come back. It may even come down to the people that we feel caused the damage within us, are still very present in our lives and unavoidable, therefore making healing a task that seems impossible.

We want it to go away…we want it to go away immediately and majority of the time that will not happen. Though ideal. The hard work seems tedious and redundant, maybe even ridiculous, but worth it. It's a must if we want to get to the place where we want to be spiritually and mentally, our soul self. Feeling and healing must happen. Drowning must occur. You must sit in the silence, be in the isolation and become one with the stillness in order to work through what you are feeling and take your control back. All in all, you are the captain of this ship and what you say and feel goes. How are you taking your power back?

Self-Guide

Questions:

> Do you feel that you are making progress towards your healing?
> Have you noticed any changes since beginning your healing process?
> How are you dealing with feeling all your emotions in a healthy way?
> Have you forgiven yourself?

Homework:

> Get a piece of paper and on one side write the situations you are still holding on to and on the other side write down how they made/make you feel
> Write a letter to the person or situation about how it made you feel. Then burn it.
> When the moment comes and you are feeling heavy emotions…feel them and if you can, record them in that moment, then go back and listen to any triggers you may have mentioned.
> Talk to someone about what happened and if trusted, receive their input.
> Take plenty of cleansing baths with sea salt.
> If possible and if you're comfortable, talk to some of the people that were involved verbally, without tension. If there is tension, leave it alone or come back to it another time.

Affirmations:
I am healed.
I am in control of my emotions
I am the creator of my future
The past is the past and I am healed from it
I grow daily towards who I desire to be
I forgive everything that happened for me
I love myself more and more everyday

"

A man who is unconscious of himself acts in a blind, instinctive way and is in addition fooled by all the illusions that arise when he sees everything that he is not conscious of in himself coming to meet him from outside as projections upon his neighbor.

"THE PHILOSOPHICAL TREE"
(1945). IN CW 13:
ALCHEMICAL STUDIES.
P.335

CYCLES

There are certain patterns that occur in our life that continue to show up repeatedly. This goes for people, situations, emotions, etc. They tend to show face so often that eventually it becomes a part of our everyday life, without the intention of doing so. These are the patterns you should be paying close attention to and focusing on more in depth. They will assist in highlighting the shadow in your life, making sure its presence is loud and clear, pointing out where you need the assistance, where you need the growth and the triggers that cause you to relapse into these old emotions. This is the time where you look to the behavior and movements of others and pinpoint where they may have influenced your thoughts or may have had an impact on how you grew into the adult you are and how you began reacting to certain circumstances.

While doing this, it's smart to understand that they did their best. The people that came into your life were taught or seen specific behaviors and unintentionally passed them down to their offspring, unknowingly sending generation after generation into a viscous, unhealthy cycle of some form of abuse. Personalities, how to raise children, how to act and react, etc., are all hand-me-downs from our oldest living or transitioned relatives. None of the characteristics of which we developed solely on our own, unless we knew otherwise. This happens continuously until the cycle is broken and the generational curse is stopped indefinitely. Unhealthy patterns aren't necessarily taught but mimicked. The people that we feel caused this damage aren't always aware that their behaviors are unhealthy and damaging to our mental and could be triggering when brought up in other situations. The patterns that these individuals are repeating are behaviors that were more than likely done to them, it's the only thing they know, so they pass it along to their sons and daughters and they pass it to their sons and daughters and the cycle continues until it is broken. The patterns and cycles that seem to bombard us can truly be healed and halted if the shadow work is done and done consistently and with love. So, when we see these patterns show up, this is when we make the right steps in becoming aware of them and noticing our part in it as well as others involved. This is where the rebuilding begins; we take the situation a part, break it down piece by piece, ask the important questions, speak with the right people and get the answers that we feel we need in order to move past this point. If we don't, the cycle will continue and will be passed down repeatedly until someone breaks it.

That someone, is you! We have future children and discoveries that will not function properly if we do not put in the work now. In order to reach the people we want to reach and heal the people we want to heal; we must first heal ourselves. Doing this includes recognizing the triggers within ourselves and the patterns that keep showing up and doing something about it. Let's stop becoming the people and family members we never wanted to be and become who we know the world needs. Generations behind us need a better understanding of self-love and healthy relationships. Do the work or continue on the hamster wheel. The choice is yours.

Self-Guide

Questions:

- ➢ What patterns do you see repeating themselves in your life?
- ➢ What do you struggle with the most in your life?
- ➢ What pieces of your personality formed from the situations you were in?
- ➢ How does it make you feel when a pattern shows up in your life that is unhealthy?
- ➢ If you have children, have you seen yourself mimicking how your parents raised you?

Homework:

- ➢ Write a list of the patterns you see that show up in your life often.
- ➢ Write what you can change or do differently to break those patterns.
- ➢ Write sticky note reminders of what unhealthy habits you are changing and keep them in a space you will see them often.

Affirmations:

I am breaking generational cycles.
I am my ancestor's proudest achievement.
I create new ways to think and react.
I respond with love.
I am receiving of love.
I deserve a life that is peaceful and tranquil.
I love everyone around me, no matter what.
I love myself and what my soul has grown into.

66

"Most of the shadows of this life are caused by standing in one's own sunshine."

RALPH WALDO EMERSON

F O R G I V E N E S S

We all tend to find this topic a bit challenging. It can be a tough one to give attention to because most of us feel like we should not be doing the forgiving but the other way around. Torture is the outcome of not forgiving someone or something. Torture to who? Well, when we don't forgive someone and the situation still exist, it's you you're torturing. You're waiting and waiting for so long for an apology from someone, that it's you that loses sleep and you who still feels the negative effects from it, the other person, sleeps like a baby. Not forgiving someone for what they have done can be triggering when we think about the situation throughout our normal day. Imagine having a conversation with someone and they say or do something that brings up an unpleasant memory, how did it make you feel? Do you notice that not only does the situation and everything tied to it bring up old feelings and emotions but now you have a shield up and can be triggered by a mere conversation from someone who may be a total stranger. We become stubborn and begin to refuse forgiving another person unless they take matters into their own hands first, because it's their fault any way, right? Wrong, forgiveness, whether it comes with an apology from another person or not, is for your benefit and no one else's. When conducting shadow work, forgiveness is in the top 3 most important tasks to achieve. It's a crucial part of your growth into a healthy, well-balanced being.

Perhaps you can look at it from a perspective of the person being totally unaware of the hurt and pain they may have caused. Is it your job to drill into their head how they made you feel or how you turned out damaged due to their actions? They have flowed into your space and acted accordingly, and it could very well be that they came for that one specific reason. This is how lessons come in to prepare us for life. We have these expectations as children that everyone is there to love us and give us room to feel safe and protected. It comes easy for some children to trust the adults that are in their lives, even if they are present with ill intentions or there for a future lesson that is to be learned. There is a lesson in everything you do and everyone who crosses your path. How will you handle them?

Forgiving someone should be the close of that chapter. No longer allow it to impact your life and give yourself permission to let it go because after this is done, all things will be new. Nothing has happened to you but for you, remember this when you lose sight of the objective. Everything that we have deemed bad or tragic have all been things that have pushed us closer to God, closer to ourselves and closer to our souls' purpose.

Self-Guide

Questions:

- ➢ Have you forgiven any of the situations or people that you feel have impacted your life? Why or Why not?
- ➢ Do you find forgiveness challenging?
- ➢ Have you forgiven yourself?
- ➢ How long have you or do you hold grudges? Is it beneficial?
- ➢ Have you noticed your toxic traits and when they show face?

Homework:

- ➢ Close your eyes and use your mind's eye to see the person you want to forgive in front of you, repeat "I forgive you" for 21 sec 3x with a 5 second break in between
- ➢ Write a letter to all the people you need and want to forgive. Trash it, burn it or give it to them.
- ➢ Light white candles and sit quietly for 5-10 minutes visualizing a life without grudges or holds, think of being free from all the pain.

Affirmations:

I forgive everything that has happened in my life
I forgive the people who have hurt me
I can change my mindset
I am the controller of my thoughts
I forgive and I am forgiven

66

"The abyss you stare into and that stares back at you is your reflection in the mirror - we all have it — that shadow self - that dark heart."

JOHN J. GEDDES

R E F L E C T I O N

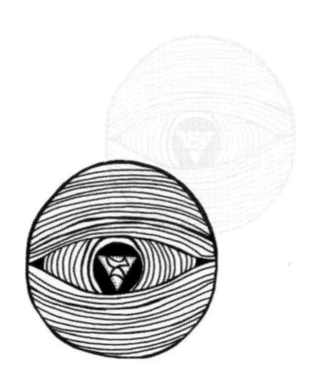

It has been about 10 chapters since we began our journey towards healing the shadow and reconnecting with our past in order to evolve it into its next timeline. There have probably been many tears shed and you've probably thrown this book across the room, but you always came back, because you were aware of its importance. You were aware that you need the darkness in order to achieve the healing you seek. There should have also been a great deal of reflecting. Reflecting on our roles in the situations and how the experiences and people have impacted our adulthood. You've also probably felt a great deal of discomfort. When coming to terms with who we are and why we are, it's easy to slip into a period of being uncomfortable with yourself and/or environment. We must begin questioning our logic against our desired immediate emotions, our defense mechanisms.

Within this chapter we will be taking somewhat of a break, a step back to look from the outside in at our current growth.   We are over halfway done with the work, but there's more to come and it is guaranteed to continue, even after the conclusion of this book. However, you do deserve some recognition for being one step closer to the closure you may have felt you needed, closer to closing the doors of childhood trauma that may have been left open unknowingly; and ultimately closer to your heightened awareness of your actions and reactions and coping and defense mechanisms, in short, your healing. This is the period of reflection, the time to ask yourself questions and be open to receiving answers.

> What lessons have I learned?
> What feelings came up that were new or noticeable?
> What lessons have come up and how have you handled them now knowing what I know?
> How have I communicated with others in my life that may have taken part in my childhood experiences?
> What situations and what deep, underlying thoughts have come to the light?
> What role did I play in the situations?
> How has this led me to showcasing my own toxic behaviors?
> How does your physical body feel after reacting on a given situation?

Many of which you can answer, will be answered or already have been answered for you as you've been journaling throughout this workbook. The most important question to ask during this period of reflection is have you been honest with yourself throughout your shadow healing journey? Have you seen what childhood traumas have impacted the way you are as an adult and how they have shaped who you are as a person and how you react to situations? How you love and flow through relationships is an outcome of who you are and your experiences. If these experiences aren't so great, neither will the relationships be, unless the shadow is seen and healed. Being honest with yourself is vital because it shows how committed you are to your healing and growth. Take a moment and analyze your honesty levels with yourself. Are you denying anything? Are you admitting that majority of the things that happened to you have affected you and perhaps even shaped who you are right this second?

Perhaps share your feelings and thoughts with another person. How your journey is going, what you've learned and how it is projecting you into the life you deserve and dream of. Think about others on this journey, if anyone else out there could use the guidance and advice, give it to them. Start a chain reaction of healing childhood trauma so that it reaches millions and has a significant effect on the generations that we precede. Spread the word that healing does not come over night, it will not be easy, it will get ugly and it will be triggering, but it's damn worth it. Childhood trauma is not the driver on this path towards enlightenment, you are.

Sit. Go Inward. Reflect.

Reassure the child in you that is yourself, that everything that happened for you, happened for a reason, as cliché as it may be, it was the path we had to go down to reach our full potential and knowledge of self.

Self-Guide

Questions:
Pg. 46

Homework:

➤ Meditate starting at 5 min and working way up to 30 min, this can be a walking, dancing, shopping, creative meditation as well.
➤ Listen to 432 Hz music for healing, DNA activation, mental blockages, letting go of negative energy.

Here are some other healing frequencies to listen to as well.

174Hz - removes pain
285Hz - Influence energy fields
396Hz - liberating guilt and fear
417Hz - undoing situations and facilitating change
528Hz - transformation and miracles (DNA repair)
639Hz - connecting/relationships
741Hz - expression/solutions
852 Hz - returning to spiritual order
963Hz - connection to the cosmos; awakening
7.83Hz - Earth's healing frequency or Schumann resonance, for grounding meditation and connecting with mother Earth
126Hz - stimulate the heart, perfect for meditation, the OM tone, frequency of the sun.

➤ Take spiritual baths for relaxation and relief

Affirmations:

I am healed.
I am understanding
I am forgiving
I am attracted to my healing

"What men call the shadow of the body is not the shadow of the body, but is the body of the soul."

OSCAR WILDE

C O M P A S S I O N

CHAPTER 12

CHAPTER 12

This can very easily turn into a time where we lack compassion for ourselves, and the love that we thought we gave shows its true colors and proves that we actually give ourselves a great deal of hate. Compassion is important during the shadow work process because we go through a phase of self-blaming for the experiences we had, unintentionally feeling like that's what we deserved. We may go through spurts of placing the blame on ourselves even if we didn't play a vital role. Some of us so easily fall into the role of the victim and allow it to coddle us like a child and we completely lose a sense of who we are in those moments. We revert to our childhood ways and our ways of wanting someone to comfort us when things are not going the way we would prefer them to go. Victimization at its finest. In adulthood, it cannot and will not always be that way. We have to show this sort of compassion to ourselves in a way that is mature and delicate, yet stern; because we can be hard on ourselves going through this journey of healing childhood trauma, but we must remember that we are taking control back into our hands. Voices may speak to us through our thoughts, telling us it's all our fault, we did this to ourselves, and so on, and if negative, they aren't always ours (careful of the company you keep). Therefore, keeping the compassion we have for our situations and experiences is necessary, so we don't stray away from the true purpose of healing.

During this chapter, accept that you are human, and you deserve the love you would give the younger version of yourself, but twice as much. Show yourself the love and care that you so desperately sought out and wallow in it. Remember that error is ok, we aren't placed on this planet to be perfect nor is it an expectation of source. We are students of life; Earth is our classroom and the soul wants to learn how to heal. Mistakes are meant to be made and the things we go through were placed in our lives for a divine purpose. Adversities shine light on how strong and resilient we are coming through situations that during them, we didn't think we'd survive.

Love yourself amidst the darkness. When you are writing the letters, answering the questions and doing all the necessary work, it must be done with love and understanding because of the intensity of their impact on our emotions. Keep yourself as your priority and take care of you during this time of deep healing and cleansing.

Self-Guide

Questions:

- ➢ Has this journey been challenging for you?
- ➢ Have you been kind to yourself during this time?
- ➢ What feelings have you had towards yourself?
- ➢ Do you find it difficult to be compassionate towards yourself?
- ➢ Even through your involvement did you or do you still have genuine love for yourself?
- ➢ Have you shown compassion towards the people that were a part of the trauma? No matter their role?
- ➢ Have you developed an understanding of the situations and why things happened the way they did?

Homework:

- ➢ Take 1-3 days for some deep self-care.
- ➢ Disconnect from the world.
- ➢ Do a social media cleanse.
- ➢ Spend time doing things you love.

Affirmations:

I am compassionate
I am kind
I love myself
I am worthy
I am beautiful
I have power and control over my emotions
I allow myself to feel
I am

"

"The person you call an enemy
is an exaggerated aspect of your
own shadow self."

DEEPAK CHOPRA

TRANQUILITY

CHAPTER 13

CHAPTER 13

How are you feeling? Do you feel like you've made it? Like you've accomplished something great? Like you've stuck to your vow, to your commitment, and to yourself? You may feel lighter, more aware, or even like a whole new being! If you feel you have succeeded in completing the last 12 chapters, at this point you should feel a sense of relief and weightlessness. You have just released an enormous amount of baggage that you once held on to so tightly, allowing it to control your every move unintentionally and to make you into the person you never wanted to be but were slowly becoming. You should now feel that you are in a state of bliss and tranquility. Not because life should be perfect now, but because you know how to maneuver it and give it attention and love as you see fit. You are now aware of your actions and reactions and any toxic behaviors you may have taken on. At this point, giving yourself love and compassion is an absolute must. You've purged so many things and flowed through many emotions that got you here. There should be enough knowledge imbedded in you now that you can begin to share your healing and tell of the powerful benefits of shadow work. You can now take the lead as the teacher or guide and show others up the path that you have successfully walked. Exhibit and give the love that you knew you needed during your healing and pass along Momentum to anyone whom you think needs that extra push to get the fire started.

Do this exercise:

Imagine yourself walking into an all-white room, top to bottom. Filled with white flowers, white birds, white drapes, waterfalls, etc. There is a quietness that is so still, that you can hear the organs in your body keeping you alive. They thank you for going through the long nights and heavy days in order to heal what they love so much, you. This is your place of tranquility, where you can now let go and breathe peacefully. You can now step into your dreams and goals full force and plan your life how you want and combat any lessons that will come your way. If you have reached this point and your healing has been obviously significant, you've made it. However, if you haven't, this isn't the end. Keep trying, keep going, do not give up; these are crucial times and if you want the life you so desperately dream of, the work must be done. If you try to avoid it out of fear that you will not be successful, you've already failed, and your shadow will continue to follow you until you face it.

In order to heal others with the services we provide and the gifts we bless the world with, we must look in the mirror first. The healing affect is a chain reaction. We all want to see the world in a better state than it is now. We wallow in the thought of how it could be; but it starts with us. One by one.

Release the trauma. Heal the world. You are the guide. You are the Momentum.

Self-Guide

Questions:

- ➤ How do you feel now that you've made it to the end?
- ➤ Did you complete all 11 chapters and assignments?
- ➤ Do you feel relieved?
- ➤ What lessons have you learned?
- ➤ What have you learned about yourself?
- ➤ Have you shared your journey with anyone else?
- ➤ Do you feel you are ready to live the rest of your life?
- ➤ Do you feel you can take on any lesson now with love and understanding?

Homework:

- ➤ Write a thank you letter to yourself.

Affirmations:

I am healed
I am healed
I am healed.

"The brightest flame casts
the darkest shadow."

GEORGE R. R. MARTIN

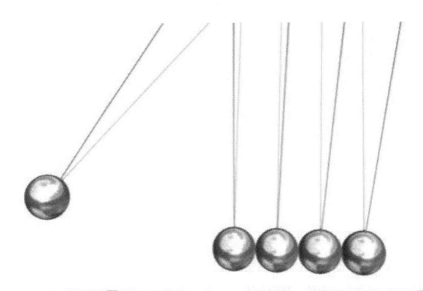

SHADOW WORK RESOURCES

HEALING IS THE THOUGHT, AWARENESS IS THE ANSWER

QUINN BARBOUR

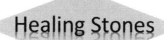

Healing Stones

Carnelian
Aids in taking bold action | helps balance sexual energy | boosts courage and self-confidence | purifies blood | improves circulation | *Root Chakra*

Amethyst
Protective stone | purifying the mind | clearing negative thoughts (*stress & anxiety*) | work related stress | abundance | family bonding | open communication | making tough work choices | *Crown Chakra*

Rose Quartz
Love stone | helps you forgive | understand disagreements and situations from another perspective | deepen connection with partner | gentle energy | washes out toxic energies and emotions you may have trapped inside you | negativity will flow out as pure thoughts of love flow in | dispelling feelings of fear and suspension that poison outlook | *Heart Chakra*

Peridot
Increase mental focus | strength to persevere | wonderful for depression | sense of self-worth & motivation | feel good stone | *Heart and Solar Chakras*

Citrine
Wealth | abundance | aid in manifestation | activate imagination | enhances mental clarity | allows the flow of ideas and visualizing | raises energy | *Root, Sacral and Solar Plexus Chakras*

Smoky Quartz
Spiritual band | aid to any emotional wounds| vibrate at your fullest potential | guides you into a higher state | soothing vibes | can recognize electromagnetic and geopathic stress | grounding and detoxifying | good for tension | neutralizes negativity | *Higher Crown Chakra*

Rhodonite
Healing relationships | encourages clear communication | clear away old patterns | makes the heart grow stronger and wiser | replaces anxiety fear and anger with warm fuzzy emotions like self-worth | well-being and stability | vibrates pure love | *Heart Chakra*

Lepidolite
Bring sense of awareness keeps in mind and body balanced | anchors emotions, courage, eases anxiety | *all chakras*

Azurite

Enhance creativity | inner wisdom | boosts intuition and spiritual wisdom (keep out of sun) | *Third Eye Chakra*

Blue Lace Agate

Natural state of joy | helps us heal by opening our energy channels to unconditional love, freedom, and serenity | immediate calming influences | *Heart Chakra*

Rutilated Quartz

Powerful cleansing and purifying effects | intuition-enhancing effects | spiritual nutrition | major energy amplifier | deep cleaning (include in energy grid w/ amethyst and sodalite) | antidepressant | *Crown and Heart Chakra*

Aquamarine

Soothing unpleasant emotions | enhance feelings of peacefulness by encouraging inner strength and bravery *(great for baths)* | refreshing energy | *Heart Chakra*

Malachite

Transformation | new relationships | guardian of the heart | remove environmental pollution | antidepressant | mood stabilizer | helps bring you out of a creative rut | neutralizes any toxic energy | *Heart Chakra*

Jasper

Manifesting strength, courage and wisdom | inspire passion | motivation | like an adrenaline rush | encourage grounding and stability | *Root Chakra*

Agate

Slow and steady | brings harmony to all aspects of being | energy of water | best for seeking fortitude | use for unbalance | spiritual protection | *all chakras*

Tigers Eye

Striking a fire of passion | boost motivation, abundance and good luck | money stone | strength to stop dreaming and the courage to start living | grow change and transform | *Solar Plexus*

Amazonite

Good luck | calming and soothing energy | anti-anxiety | release toxic emotion | excellent for manifestation | brings clarity and truth | *Heart Chakra*

Black Tourmaline

Energy purifier | the bodyguard stone | absorbs electromagnetic radiation | one of the most powerful and effective crystal for anxiety | clear negativity | protect against energy vampires | grounding | *Root Chakra*

"

"To become conscious of it involves recognizing the dark aspects of the personality as present and real."

CARL JUNG

Mudras and Mantras

Mudra | A symbolic, ritualistic hand gesture used in Hindu and Buddhist ceremonies and statuary.

Acceptance Mudra

Healing | overcoming sadness, being stuck in the past
Position | fold index finger so it rests in the space between your thumb, have your thumb touch your pinky finger, make sure your thumb is resting on the nail of your pinky. | *10 min daily*

Self- Confidence Mudra (Ahamkara)

Healing | sense of peace and confidence and helps overcome fears
Position | bend index finger slightly and touch your thumb to the outside of your index finger, a little less than halfway down. keeping other fingers straight. *10 min daily*

Patience Mudra (Shuri)

Healing | stay present in the moment and evoke patience and understanding
Position | touch top of middle fingers and thumb together. *10 min daily*

Courage Mudra (Hansi)

Healing | evoke courage, fearlessness, can relieve anxiety. Helps ease feelings of loneliness and isolation. Stimulate feelings of self-love and acceptance
Position | touch the tips of all the fingers together except pinky, hold pinky out *10 min daily*

Enlightenment Mudra (Uttarabodhi)

Healing | deeper sense of spiritual awareness and consciousness, release fears or blockages and calm nerves
Position | use both hands, interlock them, keeping index fingers and thumbs straight extend touching thumbs and index fingers straight so they are opposite each other. *10 min daily*

Mantra | A word or sound repeated to aid concentration in meditation

**Notes*:*
Do the entire set
Start with first chakra
Bring attention to that area
Repeat sound 1-3 times aloud or silently

Chakra | Location | Association | Mantra

First | Base of spine | survival instincts | LAAM

Second | Sacral area | sensuality and creative inspiration| VAAM

Third | solar plexus (navel) | personal power and ego | RAAM

Fourth | center of chest | unconditional love and compassion | YAAM

Fifth | throat | creativity | HAAM

Sixth | between brows | insight inspiration | KSHAAM

Seventh | Crown or top of head | spiritual union | OMM

&breathe

66

"Shadow work is the path
of the heart warrior."

CARL JUNG

Breathing Exercises

These exercises are mainly for clearing trauma energy

1

Clear space w/ sage, lighting candles, light/soft energetic music (research healing tones and frequencies), gather any items needed for comfort

2

Begin with natural breath, figure out where your hands want to be, next to your body, palms up or one on belly and one on heart

3

Inhale deeply into your body/belly then a secondary deep inhale through your heart

4

Bring awareness to any thoughts or feelings that come up, note them, invite them to flow freely

5

Exhale out of your mouth, bringing your awareness to trusting in love and guidance

Breathe in this order: belly | heart | head | repeat 10-30 min of active breathing

6

Allow yourself to cry, scream, vocalize however you need, if messages come to you, repeat them aloud

7

When finished, lie still, you may still feel tingling, tightness in hands, or a sense of mild physical exhaustion, all are temporary and are signs that you moved something around.

8

You may be sensitive after, avoid substances and loud noise and bright light, treat yourself with reverence to keep energy flowing

9

Pay attention to what appears in your dreams

10

Give thanks!

"The rewards are profound. Shadow work enables us to alter our self sabotaging behavior so that we can achieve a more self-directed life."

CONNIE ZWEIG

Great Escapes in Your State

Alabama

- Little River Canyon National Preserve
- Weathington Park
- Cahaba River National Wildlife Refuge
- Ruffner Mountain Nature Preserve
- Dauphin Island
- Cheaha State Park
- Turkey Creek Natural Preserve

Alaska

- Denali National Park and Preserve
- Glacier Bay National Park
- Katmai National Park and Preserve
- Kodiak National Wildlife Refuge
- Kenai Fjords National Park
- Gates of the Arctic National Park and Preserve
- Wrangell- St. Elias National Park and Preserve
- The Chugach Mountains
- The Chilkoot Trail

Arizona

- Aravaipa Canyon
- Black River
- Blue Range Primitive Wilderness
- Grand Falls
- Mount Graham
- Riggs Flat Lake
- San Pedro River

Arkansas

- Blanchard Springs Caverns
- Buffalo National River

California

- Yosemite Fall, Yosemite National Park
- Oxnard Dunes
- Sturtevant Falls, Big Santa Anita Canyon
- Mendocino Coast
- California's Pacific Coast Highway
- Humboldt Redwoods State Park
- Joshua Tree National Park
- Big Basin Redwoods
- Pfeiffer Beach
- Glacier Point
- Lava Beds National Park
- Giant Rock in Landers
- McWay Falls
- Vernal Falls
- Monterery Beaches
- Emerald Bay
- Muir Woods
- Napa Valley
- Cathedral Park
- Mariposa

Colorado

- Conundrum Hot Springs
- The Springs Resort
- Last Dollar Road
- Molas Lake Park & Campground
- Boulder Creek
- Mesa Winds Farm and Winery
- 5-star salt caves
- Trail 403

Connecticut

- Cathedral Pines Preserve
- Garden of Ideas
- Enders Falls
- White Memorial Conservation Center
- Outer Island
- Saville Dam
- Tod's Point
- Steep Rock Preserve
- Barn Island Wildlife Management Area

Delaware

- Delaware Seashore State Park
- Holts Landing
- Auburn Heights Preserve
- Bombay Hook National Wildlife Refuge
- Bowers Beach
- Assawoman Bay Wildlife Management area
- Mt. Cuba Center
- Prime hook Wildlife Refuge
- White clay creek state park

Florida

- Sanibel Island
- Ichetucknee Springs State Park
- Fort Walton beach
- Corkscrew swamp sanctuary
- Blue Spring State Park
- Naples Beach and Pier
- Crystal River
- Amelia Island
- Falling waters State Park

Georgia

- Tallulah Gorge
- Lullwater Park
- Callaway Gardens
- Panther Creek Falls
- Morningside Nature Preserve
- Etowah Indian Mounds
- Montaluce Winery
- Okefenokee Swamp
- Providence Canyon State Park
- Cumberland Island
- Roswell Falls
- Stone Mountain Park

Hawaii

- Kauapea, Kauai
- Waipio Valley Beach
- Makua Beach
- Kawakiu Beach
- Polihua Beach
- Honokalani Beach
- Harold L. Lyon Arboretum
- Makauwahi Cave
- Dragon's Teeth
- Keahiakawelo (Garden of the Gods)
- Mo'omomi Preserve
- Hunakai Beach

Idaho

- Sur Valley
- Coeur d'Alene
- Shoshone Falls
- Bruneau Sand Dunes
- Craters of the moon
- Thousand Springs
- Sandpoint
- rolling hills of the Palouse
- Sawtooth Mountains and Stanley
- Hells Canyon

Illinois

- Anderson Japanese Gardens
- The Waterfalls at Starved Rock State Park
- Burden Falls
- Fabyan Windmill at Fabyan Forest Preserve
- Ghokia Mounds
- Garden of the Gods
- Nicholas Conservatory and Gardens
- Spoon River Valley Scenic Drive
- Buffalo Rock State Park
- Cache River Wetlands
- Lake Falls at Matthiessen State Park

- Chicago Botanic Garden
- Inspiration Point

 Indiana

- Cataract Falls
- Brown County State Park
- Kissing Bridges
- Indiana Wetland
- Turkey Run State Park
- Clifty Falls State Park
- Nappanee
- Bean Blossom
- East Pierhead Lighthouse
- Hoosier National Forest
- Lake Michigan

 Iowa

- Dubuque Arboretum and Botanical Garden
- Little House on the farm and Guest barn b&b
- Pikes Peak State park
- Reiman Gardens
- Dunnings Spring Falls
- Gnotto of the Redemption
- Maquoketa Caves State

Kansas

- Monument Rocks National Natural Landmark
- Mushroom Rock State Park
- Cheyenne Bottoms Wildlife Area
- Wetlands
- Flint Hills
- Geary County Lake Waterfall
- Kansas Lavender Field

Kentucky

- Baker-Bird Winery
- Grayson Lake State Park
- Short Creek Homegrown Hideaways
- Dog Slaughter Falls
- The Appalachians
- Kentucky Lake
- Pinnacles of Benea
- Red River Gorge
- Cumberland Falls

Louisiana

- Avery Island
- Chauvin Sculpture Garden
- Bayou Sauvage National Wildlife Refuge
- Louisiana Swamp
- Jungle Gardens
- Jean Lafitte National Historical Park and Preserve
- Audubon Park

Maine

- Two lights State Park
- Ogunquit Beach
- Oh My GOSH corner
- Height of Land
- Chimney Pond
- Acadia National Park
- Moosehead Lake

Maryland

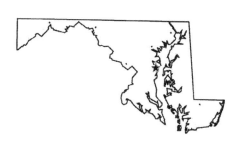

- Cunningham Falls State Park
- Baltimore Inner Harbor
- Deep Creek Lake
- Assateague Island
- Island Inn and Suites
- Janes Island State Park
- Smith Island
- Elmwood Farm Bed and Breakfast
- Matoaka Beach
- Black Walnut Point Inn

Massachusetts

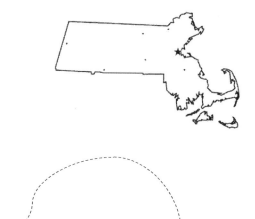

- Garden in the woods
- Heritage Museum and Gardens
- The Bridge of Flowers
- The Norman Rockwell Museum
- The Berkshire Botanical Gardens
- Sandwich Boardwalk
- Provincetown Dunes
- Nickerson State Park
- Edgar Farm
- Great Brook State Park
- Deerfield River
- BirchPond
- Old Sturbridge Village
- Breakheart Reservation

Michigan

- Tahquamenon Falls
- Suttons Bay
- Large Springs
- Kitch-iti-Kipi
- Olive Shones Beach
- Belle Isle
- Pictured Rocks National Lakeshore

- Port Austin
- Sleeping Beer Dunes National Lakeshore

Minnesota

- Boundary Waters
- Eagle Mountain
- Great River Bluff State Park
- Nerstrand Big Woods State Park
- Leif Erikson Park and Rose Garden
- Minnehaha Falls
- Itasca State Park
- Big bog State Recreation Area
- Minnesota Valley State Recreation Area
- Normandale Japanese Garden

Mississippi

- Magnolia Grove Monastery
- Sunflower Wildlife Management Area
- Clark Creek Nature Area
- Tishomingo State Park
- Little Mountain Trail
- Cypress Swamp
- Tara Wildlife
- Soul Synergy Center

Missouri

- Grand Falls
- Haha Tonka State Park
- Gothic Water Intakes
- Sandy Creek Covered Bridge
- Table Rock Lake
- Missouri Botanical Garden
- Onondaga Cave State Park
- Osage River
- Johnson's Shut-ins State Park
- Forest Park

Montana

- Flathead Lake
- Triple Divide Pass
- Goat Haunt
- Chief Mountain
- The garden of one thousand Buddhas
- Gibson Dam
- Four Dances Recreation Area
- Makoshika State Park
- Charles M Russel National Wildlife Refuge
- Calypso Trail
- Kootenai Creek
- Lomo Lake
- McDonald Lake
- Bighorn Canyon
- Medicine Rocks State Park

Nebraska

- Victoria Springs State Recreation Area
- Enders Reservoir State Recreations Area
- Gallagher Canyon State Recreation Area
- Gilman Park Arboretum
- Lord Ranch Resort
- Steer Creek Campground
- RujoDen Ranch

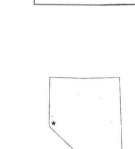

Nevada

- Valley of Fire State Park
- Mount Charleston
- Cottonwood Valley Trails
- Gardens at The Flamingo

New Hampshire

- Mount Monadnock
- Monadock Berries
- Canterbury Shaker Village
- The porches at the mountain view grand
- Franconia Notch State Park
- Conway Scenic Railroad
- New Found Lake
- Polecat Trail on Wildcat mountain

New Jersey

- The Pine Barrens
- Jenny Jump State Forest
- Parvin State Park
- Island Beach State Park
- Startswood State park
- Wildcat Ridge
- New Jersey Botanical Gardens
- Sourland Mountain Reserv

New Mexico

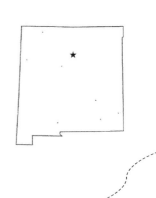

- Ghost Ranch
- Valles Caldera
- Carlsbad Caverns
- Tent Rocks
- White Sands
- Dark Skies
- Blue Hole
- Brazos Cliff
- Bandelier
- Bosque Del Apache
- Shiprock
- Gila Cliff Dwellings
- Bisti Badlands

New York

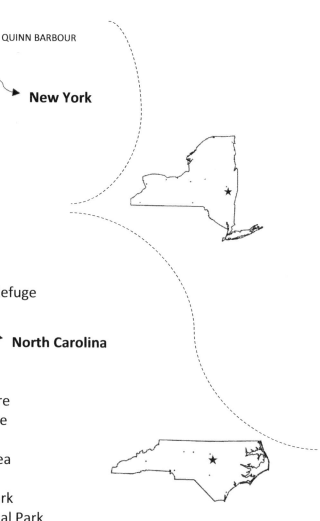

- Elevated Acre
- Inwood Hill Park
- Cloisters
- Grafton Peace Pagoda
- Mohonk Mountain House
- Sunken Forest
- Heart Island
- Havana Glen
- Montezuma National Wildlife Refuge

North Carolina

- Mount Mitchell State Park
- Cape Hatteras National Seashore
- Cape Lookout National Seashore
- Chimney Rock State Park
- Fort Fisher State Recreation Area
- Goose Creek State Park
- Grandfather Mountain State Park
- Great Smoky Mountains National Park
- Hammocks Beach State Park
- Raven Rock State Park

North Dakota

- Theodore Roosevelt National Park
- International Peace Garden
- Lake Metigoshe State Park
- Maah Daah Hey Trail
- Minot

Ohio

- Mineral Springs Lake
- Chapel Cave

- Peaceful Acres
- Mount Jeez
- Highlands Nature Sanctuary
- The Golden Bear
- Glen Helen Nature Preserve
- Edge of Appalachia Nature Preserve
- Wayne National Forest
- Nelson Kennedy Ledges State Park

Oklahoma

- Wichita Mountains Wildlife Refuge
- Quartz Mountain Resort
- Chickasaw National Recreation Park
- Natural Falls State Park
- Talimena National Scenic Byway
- Grand Lakes of the Cherokees
- Glover River
- Black Mesa Area
- Robbers Cave State Park

Oregon

- Boardman State Park
- Tulip Field
- Mount Hood
- Tumalo Falls
- Snow Lakes Trail
- The Haystack Rocks
- Toketee Falls
- Opal Creek
- Japanese Garden
- Oneonta Desert
- Thor's Well
- Umpqua Hot Springs
- Misery Ridge Hiking Trail
- Sweet Creek Trail
- Wallowa Mountains
- Yaquina Head Light and Cliffs
- Cape Meares

Pennsylvania

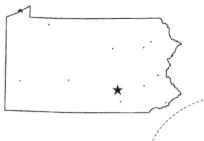

- Schenley Park
- Fairmount Park
- The Rose Garden
- Bake Oven Knob
- Presque Isle State Park
- Bushkill Falls
- Pine Creek Gorge
- Hoverter and Sholl Box Huckleberry Natural Area
- Ringing Rocks State Park
- Cherry Springs State Park

Rhode Island

- Sachuest Point
- Fort Nature Refuge
- Prudence Island
- Durfee Hill Management Area
- Burlingame State Park
- Arcadia Management Area
- Norman Bird Sanctuary
- Emilie Reucker Wildlife Refuge
- Roger Williams Botanical Center
- Neutaconkanut Park
- Quonochontaug Beach

South Carolina

- Paris Mountain State Park
- Columbia Riverfront Park and Historic Columbia Canal
- Vereen Gardens
- Table Rock State Park
- Goodale State Park
- Hopeland Gardens
- Chau Ram County
- Mount Pleasant Memorial Waterfront Park
- Lake Conestee Nature Park
- Henry C. Chambers Waterfront Park

South Dakota

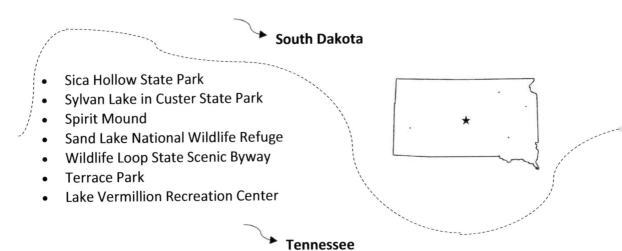

- Sica Hollow State Park
- Sylvan Lake in Custer State Park
- Spirit Mound
- Sand Lake National Wildlife Refuge
- Wildlife Loop State Scenic Byway
- Terrace Park
- Lake Vermillion Recreation Center

Tennessee

- Reelfoot Lake
- Great Smoky Mountains National Park
- Cades Cove
- Radnor Lake
- Arrington Vineyards
- Ledford Mill
- Watauga Lake
- Cherokee National Forest
- Land Between the Lakes

Texas

- Walnut Springs Park
- Boca Chica Beach
- Claiborne West Park
- Blue Hole at Riding River Ranch
- Marufo Vega Trail at Big Bend National Park
- South Llano River State Park
- Terry Hershey Park
- Levy Park
- Dragon Park
- Lakeside Park
- Secret Beach at Roy G. Guerrero Colorado River Park

Utah

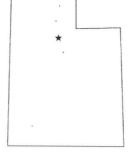

- Monument Valley
- Bryce Canyon
- Anches National Park
- Escalante National Park
- Red Cliffs
- Zion National Park
- Buckskin Gulch
- Canyonlands National Park
- Mirror Lake
- Antelope Island
- Capital Reef National Park
- Dead Horse Point State Park
- Toquerville Falls
- Lake Powell
- Alpine Loop
- Goblin Valley State Park
- Timpanogos Cave National Park

Vermont

- Lake Wiloughby
- Quechee Gorge
- Middlebury Gap Road
- Basin Harbor
- The Long Trail
- Mount Mansfield
- Groton State Park
- Lake Champlain

Virginia

- LOTUS- Light of Truth Universal Shrine
- Great Dismal Swamp and Lake Drummond
- Tangier Island
- Fairy Stone State Park
- Lewis Ginter Botanical Gardens Conservatory
- The Channels Natural Area Preserve
- Staunton River State Park
- The Jefferson Pools
- Natural Tunnel State Park

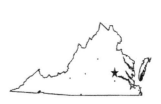

- The Devils' Bathtub
- Blue Ridge Mountains

Washington

- Ocean Shores
- Olympic National Park
- Rialto Beach
- Riverwalk Park
- Treehouse Point
- Port Townsend
- North Cascades National Park
- Port Townsend
- North Cascades National Park
- Columbia River Gorge
- La Conner

West Virginia

- Yokum's Vacation Land
- Oglebay
- Brush Creek Falls
- Harpers Ferry
- Kanawha River at Glen Ferris
- Mirror Lake
- Plum orchard Lake
- Sleepy Creek Lake
- Tygart Lake

Wisconsin

- Boynton Chapel
- Amnicon Falls State Park
- Parfrey's Glen
- Dells Mill
- Cascade Falls
- Apostle Islands Ice Caves
- Allen Centennial Gardens
- Little Manitou Falls
- Mirror Lake
- Morgan Falls
- Natural Bridge State Park

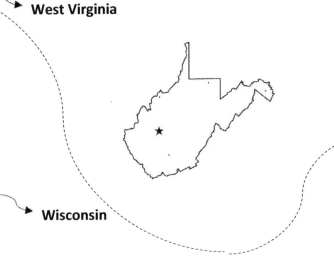

- Dave's Falls
- Thai Pavilion at Olbrich botanical Gardens
- Whitefish Dunes State Park
- Willow Falls
- Pewits Nest

Wyoming

- Killpecker Sand Dunes
- Seedskadee National Wildlife Refuge
- Crazy Woman Canyon
- Edness K Wilkins State Park
- Granite Hot Springs
- Ayres Natural Bridge
- Beartooth Pass
- Expedition island
- Flaming Gorge

66

Carl Jung called this his shadow work. He said "we never see others. Instead we see only aspects of ourselves that fall over them. Shadows. Projections. Our associations."

CHUCK PALAHNIUK

Community Mental Health Centers by State

I have complied a list of community mental health centers within each state below. I used spirit and good reviews to put together 5-10 mental health centers that you may want to utilize for your mental health needs. These are merely recommendations and if you choose to have any of these places assist you, please do your own personal research and be sure it is the best place to suit you and your needs. Do not be ashamed, we've all needed help and it's there to guide us should we see fit. Heal on.

Crisis and Suicide
Girls & Boys Town National Hotline 800-448-3000

International Suicide Hotlines
National Hopeline Network 800-SUICIDE
National Suicide Prevention Lifeline 800-273-TALK (8255)
National Youth Crisis Hotline 800-442-HOPE (4673)

Domestic Violence
National Domestic Violence Hotline (child and sexual abuse) 800-799-7233
Rape, Sexual Assault, Abuse, and Incest National Network (RAINN) 800-656-HOPE
Eating Disorders Awareness and Prevention 800-262-2463

Alabama

Birmingham Crisis Center 205-323-7777

Godsden Crisis Center 256-547-9505

Huntsville Crisis Center 256-716-1000

Crisis Center of East Alabama 334-821-8600

Mobile Helpline 251-431-5111 or 1-800-239-1117
1920 Club, 1920 10th Avenue, South Birmingham, AL 35255, 205-933-6955, *http://the1920club.com/* M-F 10-3

Cahaba Consumer Affairs, 302 Franklin Street, Selma, AL 36701, 334-418-6525, *http://cahabaconsumeraffairs.com/* M-F 1-6

SOMI Club, 4351 Midmost Drive, Mobile, AL 36609, 251-342-0261, *http://somiclub.org/* T-F 8-2
WINGS Across Alabama, 1-844-999-4647, W-S 12-8

CARESS Montgomery area peer support specialists (for addictions) 334-356-2890, mapssmgm4us@gmail.com. *www.caressinc.com*, M-F 4-8, S-S 11-7, 3447 McGehee Road

Alaska

Access Alaska- Case Management, Major Mental Illness- 800-770-4488, 121 W. Fireweed Lane. Ste 105, Anchorage, AK 99503, *www.accessalaska.org*

Alaska Mental Health Board (AMHB)- MH Planning, Coordinating, educating, advising, evaluating and advocating 800-478-6422, 431 N Franklin St. Suite 200 Juneau, AK 99801, *www.hss.state.ak.us/amhb/*

Alaska Youth and Family Network, Peer Navigation, Advocacy, Training, Recovery Management for Youth, and specialized parenting classes. 888-770-4979

Eastern Aleutian, Inc, Mental Health and Substance Abuse Telepsychiatry, 800-478-2673, Sand Point, AK 99661 *www.easternaleutiantribes.com*

Unalaskans Against Sexual Assault and Family Violence (USAFV) DV Shelter, Advocacy, 800-478-7238, 156 W. Broadway, Unalaska, AK 99685

Arizona

Peer support groups 480- 994-4407
Ed's exes eating disorder group, Peoria

West valley center for living
9745 w. Peoria Ave
Peoria 85345

HOPE (mental health)
Christ Evangelical Lutheran Church
918 S. Lithfield road. Goodyear 85338 classroom B

First light (bipolar and depression)
Lord of life Lutheran Church 13724
W Weeker Blvd, Sun City West 85375 room #1

PSA Behavioral Health Agency
2255 W Northern Ave

Phoenix 85021 Suite B100, 23rd & Northern Ave

Bipolar Bears (bipolar and depression)
St. Luke's Behavioral Health Center
1800 E. Van Buren St, Phoenix 85006,
Behavioral Auditorium

House of Umi
Herbal Apothecary
www.houseofumi.co

Arkansas

Little Rock community mental health center
1100 N University Ave #200, Little Rock, Arkansas 72207
501-686-9300

Pinnacle house at Little Rock community mental health center
1020 W Daisy L Gatson Bates Dr. Little Rock, AR 72202
501-686-9300

Mid-South Health Systems
2707 Browns Lane
Jonesboro, AR 72401
870-972-4000

California

Man Therapy *http://mantherapy.org/#/center*

7 cups *https://www.7cups.com/*

24/7 Text Line Text MHA to 741741

African American mental health resources (each mind matters)
https://www.eachmindmatters.org/mental-health/diverse-communities/africanamerican/

California suicide hotlines
http://www.suicide.org/hotlines/california-suicide-hotlines.html

Young Minds Advocacy *https://www.ymadvocacy.org*

Trevor Project (lgbtq)
https://www.thetrevorproject.org

Talkspace
https://www.talkspace.com/

California Task Force on the Status of Maternal Mental Health Care
https://www.2020mom.org/ca-task-force/

Text to 838255 National Suicide Prevention

Youth Crisis Line (text/talk/chat) (800)-843-5200

Colorado

Colorado Crisis Services (phone, text, online, walk-ins)
1-844-493-8255 text "TALK" to 38255

Safe2Tell 1-877-542-7233

Pro Bono Mental Health and Counseling Program
1-844-380-6355

Aurora Mental Health Center 11059 E Bethany Drive
Suite 200 Aurora, CO 80014
303-617-2300

Jefferson Center for Mental Health
5801 W Alameda Ave.
Lakewood, CO 80226
303-425-0300

Aurora Strong Resilience Center
1298 Peoria St.
Aurora, CO 80011
303-617-2300

Glass Hearts
P.O. Box 740988
Arvada, CO 80006
303-260-9351

Connecticut

BHCare outpatient clinic/services: Community Mental Health Authorities
203-736-2601
435 East Main Street

Ansonia, CT 06401
Serious psychiatric disabilities 18 and older

Bridges Healthcare Inc. West Haven Satellite office:
Community Mental Health Authorities
203-937-7777
270 Center Street, West Haven, CT 06516
Serious Psychiatric Disabilities

Bridges Healthcare Inc. Community Mental Health Authorities
203-878-6365
949 Bridgeport Ave
Milford, CT 06460

Community Health Resources: community mental health Authorities
Bloomfield-860-243-6584
693 Bloomfield Ave Suite 101

Enfield- 860-253-5020 ext. 139
153 Hazard Ave, Enfield, CT 06082

Manchester- 860-646-3888
444 Center Street
Manchester, CT 06040

United-Services: Community Mental Health Authorities
860-774-2020
1007 North Main Street
Dayville, CT 06241

Intercommunity, Inc: Community Mental Health Authorities
860-569-5900
111 Founders Plaza, 18th Floor East Hartford, CT

Delaware

Brandywine Counseling and Community Services
Alpha program agency: Brandywine Counseling and community Services
www.brandywinecounseling.org
2500 W Fourth Street
Wilmington, DE 19805
302-472-0381

Brandywine Counseling and Community Services
Anchor program Agency
Client centered counseling for any mental health concerns
2500 W Fourth Street
Wilmington, DE
302-225-9986

Community Mental Health Center
Wilmington Agency Division of Substance Abuse and Mental Health
www.dhss.delaware.gov/main/
Wilmington, DE 19805 302-778-6900

Connections Integrated Health and Mental Clinic
Connections community support programs Inc.
Walk in clinic
www.connectionscsp.org
500 West 8th Street
Wilmington, DE 19801
302-656-8326

Florida

Mental Health Association of Central Florida
1565 East Robinson Street
Orlando, FL 32801
407-898-0110

Sylvia Brafman Mental Health Center
6555 Power line Road
Ft. Lauderdale, FL 33309
866-756-4673

Mental Health Association of Central Florida
1525 E Robinson Street
Orlando, FL 32801
407-898-0110

Mental Health Resource Center
4080 Woodcock Drive #105

Jackson, FL 32207
904-326-3370

Georgia

Advantage Behavioral Health
834 State Hwy 11, Monroe, GA 30655
770-267-8302

Georgia Behavioral Health Professionals of Cumming
5965 Pkwy N Blvd Suite C
Cumming, GA 30040
770-886-5700

River Edge Behavioral Health
265 Boulevard NE, Atlanta, GA 30312
404-665-8600

Avita Community Partners
Youth Services
113 Bradford Street NE Gainesville, GA 30501
678-513-5800

Georgia Behavioral Health Professionals of Smyrna
400 Technology Ct SE
Smyrna, GA 30082
770-431-2354

Care and Counseling Center of Georgia
1814 Clairmont Road
Decatur, GA 30033
404 636-1457

Helping Hands Community Based Services
5524 Old National Hwy
College Park, GA 30349
404-763-8555

Hillside
690 Courtenay Dr. NE Atlanta, GA 30306
404-875-4551

Hawaii

Kauai Community Mental Health
4370 Kuhio Hwy #3 211, Lihue, HI 96766
Lihue, Hawaii 808-274-3190

Maui Youth and Family Services Inc
1931 Baldwin Ave, Makawao, HI 96768
Haliimaile, HI 808-579-8414

Hawaii Behavioral Health LLC
1330 Ala Moana Blvd Suite 1, Honolulu, HI 96814
808-585-1424

Lana'i Community Health Center
333 6th St, Lanai City, HI 96763
808-565-6919
https://lanaihealth.org

North Shore Mental Health
302 California Ave #212
Wahiawa, HI 96786
808-628-9240

West Maui Counseling Center
727 Waine'e St. #201, Lahaina, HI 96761
808-280-4192

Helping Hands Hawaii
2100 N Nimitz Hwy
Honolulu, HI 96819
808-536-7234

North Shore Mental Health Philosophy
56117 Pualalea Street
Kahuku, HI 96731
808-638-8700
www.northshorementalhealth.com

Idaho

North Idaho Community Mental Health
1717 W Ontario St. Sandpoint, ID 83864
208-265-6798

Sullivan Mental Health Services
1904 Jennie Lee Drive Idaho Falls, ID 83404
208-523-1558

Reliance Mental Health Services
447 Park Ave Idaho Falls, ID 83402
208-525-8339

Community Support Center
2035, 706 N Orchard St. Boise, ID 83706
208-429-0330

Tueller Counseling Services
2275 W Broadway Street #G Idaho Falls, ID 83402
208-524-7400

Illinois

Community Counseling Centers of Chicago
2542 W North Ave Chicago, IL 60647
c4chicago.org 773-365-7277

Robert Young Center - Community Support Program
2200 3rd Ave. Rock Island, IL 61201
unitypoint.org 309-779-2094

Pillars Community Health- The Filmore Center
6918 Windsor Ave. Berwyn, IL 60402
pillarscommunityhealth.org
708-745-5277

Human Service Center -Community Crisis Center
130 North Richard Pryor Place
Peoria, IL 61605
hscpeoria.org 309-671-8094

Community Hope and Recovery Center
121 E 2nd St. Beardstown, IL 62618
217-323-2980

Indiana

Community Mental Health Center, Inc
215 E George St. Batesville, IN 47006
amhcinc.org 812-934-4210

Indiana Council of Community Mental Health Centers, Inc
101 W Ohio St. #610, Indianapolis, IN 46204
Indianacouncil.org 317-684-3684

Community Mental Health Center
9127 Oxford Pike #A Brookville, IN 47012
cmhcinc.org 765-647-4173

Eskenazi Health Midtown Community Mental Health Wright James J. Center
1700 N Illinois St. Indianapolis, IN 46202
eskenazihealth.edu 317-880-8491

Midtown Community Mental Health Meridian Center
832 N Meridian St. Indianapolis, IN 46204
317-686-5634

Iowa

Vera French Community Mental Center
1441 W Central Park Ave. Davenport, IA 52804
verafrenchmhc.org 563-383-1900

Abbe Center for Community Mental Health
1039 Arthur St. Iowa City, IA 52240
abbemhc.org 319-338-7884

Plains Area Mental Health Center
515 IA-39 Denison, IA 51442
plainsareamentalhealth.org
712-263-3172

Community Health Center-Southern
221 E State St. Centerville, IA 52544
chcsi.org 641-856-6471

Everly Ball Community Mental Health
945 19th St. Des Moines, IA 50314
everlyball.org 515-241-0982

Kansas

Bert Nash Community Mental Health Center
200 Maine St. Lawrence, KS 66044
bertnash.org 785-843-9192

Johnson County Mental Health Center
1125 W Spruce St. Olathe, KS 66061
jocogov.org 913-826-4200

COMCARE Community Crisis Center
635 N Main St. Wichita, KS 67203
sedgwickcounty.org 316-660-7500

Four County Mental Health Center
1601 W 4th St. Coffeyville, KS 67337
fourcounty.com 620-251-8180

Crawford Mental Health
3101 N Michigan St. Pittsburg, KS 66762
crawfordmentalhealth.org 620-231-5130

Kentucky

Kentucky River Community Care: Perry County Outpatient
115 Rockwood Ln, Hazard, KY 41701
606-436-5761

Comprehensive Care Center
1351 Newtown Pike #5 Lexington, KY 40511
859-253-1686

Communicare Inc.
324 E Main St. Springfield, KY 40069
859-336-7746

North Key Community Care
7075 Industrial Rd. Florence, KY 41042
859-282-1770

North Key Community Care
7959 Burlington Pike, Florence, KY 41042
859-283-9222

Louisiana

Women's Community Rehabilitation Center
855 St. Ferdinand St. Baton Rouge, LA 70802
225-336-0000

Community Care Solutions
200 S Brood Ave. #7 New Orleans, LA 70119
504-309-9991

Lake Charles Mental Health Center
4105 Kirkman St. Lake Charles, LA 70607
337-475-8022

Gonzales Mental Health Center
1112 E Ascension Complex Blvd., Gonzales, LA 70737
225-621-5770

Maine

Dorothea Dix Psychiatric Center
656 State St. Bangor, ME 04401
207-941-4000

Common Ties Mental Health Services
12 Bates St. Lewiston, ME 04240
207-795-6710

Maine Medical Center Outpatient Psychiatry- Mcgeachey Hall
216 Vaughan St. Portland, ME 04102

Maryland

Mosaic Community Services Outpatient Mental Health Clinic
2225 N Charles St. 1st Floor, Baltimore, MD 21218
443-683-8055

Upper Shore Community Mental Health Center
300 Scheeler Road, Chestertown, MD 21620
410-778-5783

The Mental Health Center
1180 Professional Ct. Hagerstown, MD 21740
301-791-3045

Oasis: The center for mental health
175 Admiral Cochrane Drive Annapolis, MD 21401
410-571-0888

The Maryland Centers for Psychiatry
2525 Riva Road. Annapolis, MD 21401
410-266-9230

Massachusetts

Massachusetts Mental Health Center
75 Ferwood Road, Boston, MA 02115
617-626-9300

South Bay Community Services
Dowling Building Co
22 Pleasant St. #2000, Malden, MA 02148
781-851-2648

The Brookline Center for Community Mental Health
41 Garrison Road, Brookline, MA 02445
617-277-8107

South Bay Community Services
541 Main St. #303, South Weymouth, MA 02190
781-331-7866

Michigan

Detroit East Community Mental Health Center
11457 Shoemaker St. Detroit, MI 48213
313-331-3435

North County Community Mental Health
105 Hall Street, Traverse City, MI 49684
231-922-4850

204 Meadows Drive
Grayling, MI 49738
989-348-8522

2715 South Townline Road
Houghton Lake, MI 48629
989-366-8550

527 Cobb Street
Cadillac, MI 49601
231-775-3463

Minnesota

Avivo
1825 Chicago Ave, Minneapolis, MN 55404
612-752-8200

Ramsey County Mental Health
1919 University Ave W #200 St. Paul, MN 55104
651-266-7890

Seward Community Support Program
2105 Minnehaha Ave, Minneapolis, MN 55404
612-333-0331

Lee Carlson Center for Mental Health and Well-Being Fridley Clinic
7954 University Ave. NE, Fridley, MN 55432
763-780-3036

Central Minnesota Mental Health Center
308 12th Ave S #1 Buffalo, MN 55313
736-682-4400

Minnesota Mental Health Clinics
3450 O'Leary Lane, Eagan, MN 55123
651-454-0114

Touchstone Mental Health
2312 Shelling Ave, Minneapolis, MN 55404
612-874-6409

Hope Community Support Program
157 Roosevelt Road, #300, St. Cloud, MN 56301
320-240-3324

Northwestern Mental Health Center
603 Bruce St. Crookston, MN 56716
218-281-3940

Mississippi

Weems Community Mental Health Center
355 MS-37, Raleigh, MS 39153
800-803-0245

Mississippi Department of Mental Health Center
1600 Broad Ave. Gulfport, MS 39501
228-863-1132

Gulf Coast Mental Health Center
15094 County Barn Road, Gulfport, MS 39503
228-248-0125

Missouri

Clark Community Mental Health Center
104 W Main St. Pierce City, MO 65723
917-476-1000

Community Counseling Center
402 S Silver Springs Road Cape Girordeau, MO 63703
573-334-1100

Tri-County Mental Health Services
3100 NE 83rd St. #1001, Kansas City, MO 64119
816-468-0400

Montana

Eastern Montana Community Mental Health Center
2508 Wilson St. Miles City, MT 59301
406-234-0234

Northwest Community Health Center
320 East 2nd Street
Libby, Montana 59923
406-283-6900

Nebraska

Nebraska Mental Health Center
4545 S 86th St. Lincoln, NE 68526
402-483-6990

Community Alliance
4001 Leaven Worth Street
Omaha, Nebraska 68105
402-341-5128

Bryan Health
1600 S 48th St.
Lincoln, NE 68506
402-481-1111 or 800-742-7844

Blue Valley Behavioral Health
1212 Ivy Ave. #2, Crete, NE 68333
402-826-2000

Nevada

Southern Nevada Adult Mental Health Services
East Las Vegas Clinic
1785 E Sahara Ave. suite 145, Las Vegas, NV 891051
702-486-6400

Southern Nevada Adult Mental Health Services
West Charleston Clinic
6161 W Charleston Blvd Las Vegas NV 89146
702-486-6045

Westcare Nevada Community Involvement Center
323 N Maryland Pkwy, Las Vegas, NV 89101
702-385-3330

Community Counseling Center
714 E Sahara Ave Las Vegas, NV
702-369-8700

Summit Mental Health
2810 W Charleston Blvd, #77 Las Vegas, NV 89102
702-823-3910

Together We Stand "TWS"
twscoofficemanager@gmail.com
702-808-9204

New Hampshire

The Mental Health Center of Greater Manchester
401 Cypress Street Manchester, NH 03103
603-668-4111

Greater Nashua Mental Health
603-883-1626
7 Prospect St.

*Riverbend Community Mental Counseling and Mental Health
130 Pembroke Road
Concord, NH 03301

Riverbend Community Mental Community Support Program
10 West Street
Concord, NH 03301

New Jersey

Bayonne Community Mental Health Center
601 Broadway, Bayonne, NJ 07002
201-339-9200

Richard Hall Community Mental Health
500 N Bridge St. Bridgewater Township, NJ 08807
908-725-2800

Brighter Days Community Wellness Center
268 Bennetts Mills Road, Jackson Township, NJ 08527
732-534-9960

New Mexico

New Mexico Behavioral Health
3695 Hot Springs Blvd. Las Vegas, NM 87701
505-454-2100

New Mexico Solutions
707 Broadway Blvd NE #500, Albuquerque, NM 87102
505-268-0701

Sequoya Adolescent Treatment Center
3405 Pan American fwy NE Albuquerque, NM 87107
505-222-0355

New York

Community Mental Health Center
521 Beach 20th St. Far Rockaway, NY 11691
718-869-8822

The Bridge
290 Lenox Ave 3rd floor New York, NY 10027
212-663-3000

New York State Office of Mental Health
Customer Relations
44 Holland Ave, Albany, NY 12229
1-800-597-8481

Vibrant Emotional Health Main Office
50 Broadway, Fl 19 New York, NY 10004
212-254-0333 *info@vibrant.org*

THE BRONX: NEW YORK

Einstein Community Health Outreach Clinic
1894 Walton Ave, Bronx, NY 10453
718-583-3060
www.einstein.yu.edu

Institute for Family Health: Center for Counseling
1894 Walton Ave., Bronx, NY 10453
718-583-2508

BROOKLYN: NEW YORK

Beverly Mack Harry Consulting Services
738 Crown Street, Brooklyn, NY 11213
718-363-0100
www.bmhtherapy.org

Community Counseling and Meditation Brooklyn #1
25 Elm Place, 2nd floor Brooklyn, NY 11201
718-802-0666
#2- 718-230-5100
#3- 718-935-9201

Manhattan

Bellevue/NYU Program for survivors of torture
Bellevue Hospital Center
462 First Avenue CD732
New York, NY 10016
info@survivorsoftorture.org
212-562-8713
survivorsoftorture.org

City College: The Psychological Center
365 Fifth Ave New York, NY 10016
212-650-6602

Family Health Center of Harlem
1824 Madison Ave
New York, NY 10035
212-423-4200

St. Francis Counseling Center
135 W 31st Street New York, NY 10001
212-736-8500

Sanctuary for Families
212-349-6009 Ext 221
sanctuaryforfamilies.org

QUEENS

Libertas Center
79-01 Broadway, Queens, NY 11373
718-334-6209

North Carolina

Appalachian Community Services
1482 Russ Ave. Waynesville, NC 28786
888-315-2880

Family First Community Services LLC
3705 Latrobe Dr. #340 Charlotte, NC 28211
704-364-3989

Fernandez Community Center
8376 Six Forks Rd. #104 Raleigh, NC 27615
919-900-7438

Cornerstone Community Outreach, LLC
5700 Executive Center Dr. #214 Charlotte, NC 28212

North Dakota

Community Action Partnership
202 E Villard St. Dickerson, ND 58601
701-227-0131

The Village Family Service Center
1201 25th St. S Fargo, ND 58103
701-451-4900

The Village Family Service Center
Bismarck-Tuscany Square
107 West Main Ave. Suite 350 Bismarck, ND 58501
701-255-1165

The Village Family Service Center
Devils Lake
224 4th St. NW Suite 5
Devils Lake, ND 58301
701-662-6776

The Village Family Service Center
Grand Forks
Grand Cities Mall
1726 S Washington St. Suite 33A
Grand Forks, ND 58201
701-746-4584

Ohio

Appleseed Community Mental Health Center
2233 Rocky Lane Ashland, OH 44805
419-281-3716 24-hour crisis 419-289-6111
rape crisis/DV 419-289-8085

Community Mental Healthcare, Inc
Dover Office:

201 Hospital Drive
Dover, OH 44622
330-343-6631

Carrollton Office
331 W Main St. Carrollton, OH 44615
330-627-4313

Zepf Center
905 Nebraska Ave, Toledo, OH 43607
419-841-7701

North Central Mental Health
1301 N High St. Columbus, OH 43201
614-299-6600

Mental Health Services
8315 Detroit Ave. Cleveland, OH 44102
213-243-1511

Oklahoma

Jim Taliaferro Community Mental Health Center
602 SW 38th St. Lowton, OK 73505
580-248-5780

Hope Community Services Inc
6100 S Walker Ave. Oklahoma City, OK 73139
405-634-4400

Edwin Fair Community Mental Health Center
Case Management and Medication Clinic
201 East Chestnut Ponca City, OK 74601
580-763-6059
After Hours 800-566-1343

NorthCare
2617 General Pershing Blvd, Oklahoma City, OK 73107
405-858-2700

Oregon

Clackamas County Mental Health
2051 Kaen Rd. Oregon City, OR 97045
503-655-8336

Polk County Mental Health
1520 Plaza St. NW Suite 150, Salem, OR 97304
503-585-3012

Clackamas County Urgent Mental Health
11211 SE 82nd Suite O, Portland, OR 97086
503-722-6200

Pennsylvania

Northeast Community Center
Roosevelt Blvd. and Adams Ave.
Philadelphia, PA 19124
215-831-2800

Community Connections
375 Beaver Drive Suite 100
DuBois, PA 15801
814-371-5100

CareLink Community Support Services
605 E Baltimore Pike Media, PA 19063
610-632-8156

Penndel Mental Health Center
Community Outreach and Administrative Offices
2005 Cabot Blvd West Suite 100
Langhorne, PA 19047
267-587-2300

Administrative Case Management and PATH services
215-750-9643

Rhode Island

The Providence Center
528 North Main Street Providence, RI 02904
401-276-4020

The Providence Center Adult Outpatient Services
530 North Main St. Providence, RI 02904
401-528-0110

Gateway Healthcare
249 Roosevelt Ave Suite 205
Pawtucket, RI 02860
401-724-8400

Rhode Island Free Clinic
655 Broad St. Providence, RI 02907
401-274-6347

South Carolina

Piedmont Center-Mental Health
20 Powderhorn Rd. Simpsonville, SC 29681
864-963-3421

South Carolina Dept of Mental Health
1050 Ribaut Rd Beaufort, SC 29902
843-524-3378

Spartanburg Area Mental Health Center
250 Dewey Ave. Spartanburg, SC 29303
864-585-0366

Federation of Families of SC
810 Dutch Square Blvd Suite 486
Columbia, SC 29210
803-772-5210

South Dakota

Southeastern Behavioral Health Counseling and Children Services
2000 S Summit Ave Sioux Falls, SD 57105
605-336-0510

Dakota Counseling Institute
910 West Havens Ave. Mitchell, SD 57301
605-996-9686

Bridgeway Counseling Center
600 4th St. NE Suite 203
Watertown, SD 57201

Tennessee

Quinco Mental Health
10710 Old Highway 64
Bolivan, TN 38008
731-658-6113

Alliance Healthcare Services
2579 Douglass Ave.
Memphis, TN 38114
901-369-1480

Alliance Healthcare Services
3628 Summer Ave. Memphis, TN 38122
901-452-6941

Alliance Healthcare Services
2100 Whitney Ave Memphis, TN 38127
901-353-5440

Alliance Healthcare Services
2150 Whitney Ave.
Memphis, TN 38127
901-353-5440

Alliance Healthcare Services
3810 Winchester Rd. Memphis, TN 38118
901-369-1400

Alliance Healthcare Services
1200 Peabody Ave. Memphis, TN 38104
901-707-6861

Mental Health America
446 Metroplex Dr. Suite A-224
Nashville, TN 37211
615-269-5355

Carey Counseling Center
300 Hwy 641 Camden, TN 38320
731-584-6999
Crisis Line 800-353-9918

Texas

Fayette County Mental Health Center
Bluebonnet Trails Community Services   .
1009 North Georgetown St. Round Rock, Texas 78664
512-255-1720
www.bbtrails.com

Texas Abuse Hotline
800-252-5400

Lake Regional Community Center
972-524-4159
For Emergency (Hunt, Kaufman, Rockwell Counties) 866-260-8000
(Camp, Delta, Franklin, Hopkins, Laman, Morris, and Titus Counties
877-466-0660

Coastal Plans Community Center
200 Marriott Drive, Portland, TX 78374
362-777-3991 Toll Free 1-888-819-5312

The Center for Health Care Services
6800 Park Ten Blvd Suite 200-S San Antonio, TX 78213
210-261-1250

Mental Health Connection
3200 Sanguinet St. Fortworth, TX 76107
817-927-5200

Gulf Coast Center
10000 Emmett F Lowry Suite
1220 Texas City, Texas 77591

Mental Health America of Greater Dallas
624 N. Good Latimer Exp Suite 200
Dallas, TX 75204
214-871-2420

Family Center of Galveston County
Galveston Office
2200 Market St Suite 600
Galveston, TX 77550
409-762-8636

Dickinson Office
2401 Termini Street Suite C
Dickerson, TX 77539
281-576-6366 or 409-938-4814

Utah

Wasatch Mental Health
Westpark Family Clinic and WMH Administration
750 N Freedom Blvd. Provo, UT 84601
801-373-4760
24-hour crisis 801-373-7393

Provo Family Clinic
1165 E 300 N. Provo, UT 84606
801-377-1213

Four Corners Community Behavioral Health
Price Clinic 575 E 100 S. Price
Castle Dale Clinic 45 E 100 S Castle Dale
Moab Clinic 198 E Center St. Moab
435-381-2432

Utah Valley Clinic Psychiatry and Counseling
395 W Bulldog Blvd
Provo, UT 84604
801-357-7525

Southwest Behavioral Health Center
474 W 200 N Suite 300 St. George, UT 84770
435-634-5600

Bear River Mental Health Services Inc.
Logan 90 East 200 North Logan, UT 84321
435-752-0750

Brigham City
663 West 950 South Brigham City, UT 84302
435-734-9449

Tremonton
440 West 600 North Tremonton, UT 84337
435-257-2168

Garden City
115 S Bear Lake Blvd Garden City, UT 84028
800-620-9949

Randolph
275 North Main Street
Randolph, UT 84064
800-620-9949

Vermont

Clara Martin Center
11 North Main Street Randolph, VT 05060
802-728-4466

Lamoille County Mental Health
72 Harrel Street
Morrisville, VT 05661
802-888-5026

Centerpoint Services
1025 Airport Drive
South Burlington, VT 05403

94 West Canal Street
Winooski, VT 05404

Virginia

Mount Rogers Community Services Board
770 West Ridge Road
Wytheville, VA 24382
276-223-3200

Goochland-Powhatan Community Services
Powhatan
3910 Old Buckingham Road
Powhatan, VA 23139
804-598-2200

Goochland
3058 River Road
West Goochland, VA 23063
804-556-5400

Virginia Family Services
1012 West 3rd Street, Ste J
Farmville, VA 23901
434-395-1200

Richmond
4912 West Marshall Street
Ste. C Richmond, VA 23230
804-313-6767

Eastern Shore Community Services Board
24233 Lankford Highway
Tasley, VA 23441
757-442-3636

Garthlon Center
8119 Holland Road
Alexandria, VA 22306
703-360-6910

Adult Case Management and Outpatient Services- Bristol
1969 Lee Highway
Bristol, VA 24201

Washington

Sound
6400 Southcenter Blvd
Tukwila, WA 98188
206-901-2000

Sea Mar Community Health Centers
1040 S. Henderson St. Seattle, WA 98108
425-312-0277

1920 100th St. SE Suite A2 and C3
Everett, WA 98208

Center for Human Services
Shoreline-170th
17018 15th Ave NE
Shoreline, WA 98155
206-362-7282

CHS Shoreline-148th
14803 15th Ave NE
Shoreline, WA 98155
206-362-7282

CHS Edmonds-Pacific Commons
21727 76th Ave W Suite J
Edmonds, WA 98026
206-362-7282

Comprehensive Healthcare
Yakima Center- Main Office
402 S 4th Ave
Yakima, WA 98902
509-575-4084

West Virginia

Shenandoah Community Health 99 Tavern Road
Martinsburg, WV 25401
304-263-4999

Appalachian Community Health Center
725 Yokum Street, Elkins, WV
304-636-3232

KVC West Virginia
1510 Kanawha Boulevard
East Charleston, WV 25311

Carruth Center
390 Birch Street
P.O. Box 6422 Morgantown, WV 26506

Help4WV
844-HELP4WV
text-844-435-7498
24/7/365

Wisconsin

Mental Health America
600 W Virginia St. Suite 502
Milwaukee, WI 53204
414-276-3122

Community Counseling Center
6629 University Ave Ste. 209 (2nd Floor)
Middleton, WI 53562
608-833-5880

Northlakes Community Clinic
Ashland Downtown
300 Main Street W Ashland, WI 54806
888-834-4551 or 715-685-2200

Lakewood 15397 State Highway 32
Lakewood, WI 54138
888-834-4551 or 715-276-6321

Aurora Community Services
406 Technology Drive
Menomonie, WI 54751

Wyoming

Rock Springs Community Health Center
2620 Commercial Way Suite #140
Rock Springs, WY 82901
301-212-5116

High Country Behavioral Health
Afton
389 Adams Street Afton, WI 83110
301-885-9883

Evanston
190 Overthrust Road Evanston, WY 82930
307-789-4224

Kemmerer
821 Sage Street Kemmerer, WY
307-877-4466

Pinedale
24 Country Club Lane
Pinedale, WY 82941
307-367-2111

Northern Wyoming Mental Health Center
Sheridan County Outpatient Services

1221 West 5th Street
Sheridan, WY 82801
307-674-4405

Johnson County Outpatient Services
420 Deanne Ave
Newcastle, WY 82701
307-746-4456

Weston County Outpatient Services
420 Deanne Ave
Newcastle, WY 82701
307-746-4456

Crook County Outpatient Services
4201/2 Main Street
Sundance, WY 82729
307-283-3636

66

The people who trigger us
to feel negative emotion
are messengers for the
unhealed parts of our
being.

TEAL SWAN

Homemade Healing

Meditation
Spend time w/ children you know
Write letters
Write poetry
Treat yourself
Have a ME day
Watch funny videos
Cry...hard
Vent to a listening/non-judgmental ear
Vacation to water
Do something nice for someone
Become familiar w/ healing herbs
Do something you love
Watch a cartoon/animated movie
Go to a movie
Pamper yourself
Sungaze
Dance to upbeat music
Breathing
Walk in nature
Ground barefoot
Take a shower w/ peppermint, lavender or eucalyptus
Talk through it in your head and ask yourself questions
Set the mood w/ candles
Sage your space
Do yoga
Listen to high frequency music
Spiritual bath
Exercise
Color
Create an arts and crafts piece
Learn something new
Complete a chapter of this book
Record voice memos venting
Practice sensual self-love
Incorporate CBD into your life

Journal Entries

Journal Entries

Journal Entries

Journal Entries

Journal Entries

Journal Entries

"

When you do shadow work, you are doing the work of radical self - acceptance

UNKNOWN

Printed in Poland
by Amazon Fulfillment
Poland Sp. z o.o., Wrocław

60786927R00081